The DreamWeaver

God's Plan for Releasing You into Your Dreams

Sammy Ray Scaggs

Each of us has one ... a God-given dream in our hearts of what we can become. In *The DreamWeaver*, Sam Scaggs takes us on a wonderful personal journey that begins when he is just a few days old as he rests in his grandmother's arms. Each chapter brings us to the sparkling discovery of what God has placed within us. Simple and heartfelt, Sam introduces us afresh to the Giver of dreams and the Killer of nightmares. There's no greater tomorrow than what lies in each of us today. Let the adventure begin!

Dr. Wayne Cordeiro
November 27, 2009

What Others Are Saying:

"This book is dangerous. It will ruin you for settling in for the ordinary and move you to get back in your dream adventure. Sam Scaggs is a gifted communicator and these compelling stories are a gift of inspiration to fully live out your own story. I have watched him work out this dream process for years, up close, and he and this book ring with integrity. Sam has powerfully ignited a fire of dream activation in the nations and now it is your turn to reap the benefits of his life story with *The DreamWeaver*. This message changed my life and will not leave you the same."

Dr. Joseph Umidi
Professor/Pastor/CEO

"It has been my joy to have known Sam Scaggs for the past twenty years. Forty years ago I met Charles "Tremendous" Jones and he said to me, "You will be who you are next year this time except for the people you meet and the books you read." I am better today because of Sam's investment in my life. He is my friend, we are partners in ministry and you will be better for having taken the time to read *The DreamWeaver*. May God release you into your dream is my prayer!"

Steve Wingfield
Evangelist & CEO

"Everyday, Christians around the world face tough times, personal loss and soul-trying calamity. And beyond the crisis, we face a loss of hope in the everyday reality of life's little drudgeries. A flat tire. A job performed without passion. Broken relationships. We despair to wonder, *Is this all there is?* We've heard promises of abundant life, experienced a taste of the divine, but a monument of dullness assails our feeble attempts at freedom. *The DreamWeaver* guides us back, prodding our souls with a constant beat on the drum of hope. *Dare to dream!* Capture the satisfaction of knowing you're walking a path of destiny, holding the hand of the one who created a life designed specifically for you. Experience life beyond complacent normality. Open this book and be refreshed to live, love, risk, and dream again."

Harry Kraus, MD
Missionary Surgeon and Best-Selling Author

"Sam is a story teller par excellance! This book carries a theme that inspires the heart, chapter by chapter. Weaving your dreams will take on a new significance as you read *The DreamWeaver*. I particularly liked the third chapter, *"Who's Your Daddy?"* Thanks, Sam, for the way you let Christ flow through you."

Dr. Ralph W. Neighbour, Jr.
Author & Cell Church Movement Consultant

"Sammy Ray Scaggs has captured both the father heart of God and the heart of God for fathers with breathtaking passion and purity. The world is full of ripped and twisted dreams, but none so shredded that He, *The Dream Weaver*, cannot recreate them in a tapestry of such surpassing beauty that we stand transfixed and transformed. Sammy Ray is a sure-footed, inspired guide into that "dream" world where reality reigns."

Richard Showalter
President, Eastern Mennonite Missions

Dedicated to:

The Fathers & Mothers of My Life

Jerry & Barbara Scaggs
Dad & Mom, you gave me my name and taught me
to be generous,
hospitable to guests, hard working and honest.
Your love and belief in me means more
than words can express.

Harold & Twila Buckwalter
You not only gave me your youngest daughter
to be my wife,
you adopted me into your family and demonstrated
the secrets found in this book. How can I ever thank you?

Stanley & Francis Fawley
When I am in your presence I see Jesus.
Just thinking of your love and relationship brings tears
to my eyes.
Thanks for believing in me when others could not
or would not.

Joseph & Marie Umidi
You both are my heroes and you revealed to me the
difference between
a religious leader and a genuine spiritual father
and mother.
Thanks for demonstrating the "father heart of God" and
taking the risk to give me a second chance.
I love you both!

Last but certainly not least . . .

Lebern Belmer & Alice Carol Johnson
Grandpa & Grandma, you planted the seeds of the Gospel
in my heart
and watered them. You gave me my first glimpse of
"the father heart of God"
& my "God-dream" long before I knew they existed.
I will see you both in heaven!

For Beverly Jean:
My Wife & My Dream Come True!

&

All our children and grandchildren:

Jason, Rebekah, Ethan & Joel Fulford
and
James & Sarah Winslow

The reasons I wrote these words . . .

ACKNOWLEDGMENTS

My deepest thanks to those who have helped me on this journey and put this message in your hands:

Irv & Kathy Peifer and Paul & Rachel Skilleter, thank you for providing the "place of refuge" in the mountains where 90% of this book was written. Your friendship and encouragement means so much to me.

Paul Arends, thank you for your excellent help with editing and making so many helpful suggestions.

Joseph Umidi, not only are you a father, friend and partner but you have been one of the best coaches a man could ever ask for. Thanks for your challenge to see this project through to the end. If there were more men like you this world would change rapidly for the better.

James Allen, you have always been my dream partner and encourager. Thank you for the excellent work you did on the cover design. You always could capture the images inside my head and make it possible for others to see them. You have taught me what true friendship is all about and have given me the reason to trust another man.

PROLOGUE

There are seemingly two "life messages" *"Woven Together"* within me: *Spiritual Fathering* and the *Power of Your Dreams.* Try as I have to go on to other themes, ideas and messages I just keep coming back to these two again and again. But are they both woven into one life message? You hold in your hands the answer to that question. Is it possible that God, our Heavenly Father desires for each of us as "sons and daughters" to have a life mission and that is to discover Him . . . "The DreamWeaver?"

Is it possible for us to become like Him and mature into "fathers and mothers" who are used of God to help others make that same discovery? Two men have been used of God to help me in this discovery more than others. Dr. Mark Handby, author of *"You Have Not Many Fathers"* transformed my life and sent me on a journey that I am still taking to this day, and Dr. Wayne Cordeiro has mentored me like no other in becoming a "*Dream Releaser*." It is obvious that these two leaders have deeply influenced my life, my thinking and my writing on this subject of knowing and making known to you . . . "The DreamWeaver!"

It is my prayer that as God moves over the face of this earth restoring the truth of spiritual fathers and dream releasing, many in my generation will not settle for anything less than responding to the highest calling on earth: *becoming spiritual fathers and mothers with the heart of God beating in their chests and then fulfilling THE VISION of God which is to see each and everyone of His sons and daughters unlock & release their God-dreams into the Kingdom of God!* We have settled far too long for following someone else's dream and suffered at the hands of religious leaders instead of being blessed and released to be all that God has called us to be—sons and daughters who grow up to be fathers and mothers of . . .

"The DreamWeaver!"

CONTENTS

FOREWORD

"The thief comes only to steal, and kill, and destroy;
I came that they might have life, and might have it
abundantly."
—*Jesus (John 10:10) NASB*

I t was another gorgeous day in Bari. This city was as old as the Bible but had been redesigned by Mussolini during World War II. Our doors were propped open and the Mediterranean breeze flowed through the room along with the hustle and bustle of the city below. I had only been there with my family for a few months. My long held dream had come true! I was living with my family in another country sharing the Hope that was within me! However, my palms were sweating and my heart was racing as the reality of what we were attempting to do began to sink deeply into my mind—speaking another language!

"Every Italian verb has to be conjugated 14 times. Seven singular and seven-compound," kept ringing inside my brain! I looked right into Bev's eyes and said, "Whose idea was it to come here and learn a foreign language at our age?" Knowing her answer and trying to look serious, she responds, "Yours!" Just then, the buzzer to our sixth floor apartment rang out. Our daughter, Rebekah raced across the slick Italian tile and slid to the intercom like an Olympic speed skater on her last leg of the race and shouted, "Rosa is here!"

Rosa was one of our language instructors and she was tiny in stature, sweet in personality but brutal as an instructor! Just the way I loved it! It was on this particular day we would encounter something neither of us had planned for but which would change the way I thought of God forever.

As we concluded the session I began to make jokes and conversation, only in Italian of course, because Rosa would have it no other way. I was telling her about a trip to a little "trattoria" near Brindisi, a nearby city about an hour south along the Adriatic Coast where I stepped out of my comfort zone to order some authentic Italian food for our family because there was no translator.

As we began to interact with the owner of the little bistro and his family, joy began to well up in my heart—"we can do this!" I thought to myself. Our oldest daughter trusted her instincts as she listened to my broken Italian and she ordered a small bag of popcorn and ice cream. Our youngest, Sarah, still trusted her dad and she went along with her mother and me for our quest for an authentic Italian lunch.

We ordered the works. Salad, olives, bread of course and pasta! You could smell the salt air and hear the waves crashing down upon the rocks nearby. I smiled and said to my family, "It just doesn't get any better than this!" Well, that was until the pasta arrived. I looked at the man swelled with pride as he walked up to our table carrying three plates of steaming linguini. Then my eye caught the expression of my youngest daughter. With tears swelling up in her eyes all she could say was, "I don't want that—may I have popcorn and ice cream?" I knew something was wrong!

You know the feeling when your brain hasn't caught up with an event that everyone around you is experiencing? I looked at the platter that we had all anticipated and gasped. It was white steaming linguini all right but it had something hideous on top of it. A black sea creature of some kind; with black sauce running down on all sides of it seeping deep into the white pasta! I quickly went into action (this was a family memory that was at stake here). I said, to the waiter and owner of the restaurant, "Non abbiamo ordinato questo!" (We did not order this!) His proud smiling face dropped with disappointment like I had just insulted his dead mother and he began to remind me that we had indeed ordered these plates of "sepianeri!"

Sepia! I don't recognize that word. Neri. Yes, "neri" means "black." Yes, we had figured that out just with our eyes. Sepia, oh no, my mind raced through my new list of vocabulary of Italian words, it means "squid!" I had ordered three plates of boiled squid with black sauce made from the squid's ink! I told the man that I was sure it was good but that we would need to order something else. My youngest daughter decided that she would have popcorn and ice cream and . . . I was interrupted by the gentle and sweet voice of my wife who said, "I would like to try it." The man's eyes lit up like he had seen his dead mother rise from the grave. And before I could finish my protest, my wife had the steaming plate of pasta in front of her, cut a small piece and began eating it to my horror! I could see black ink on her lips and teeth!

Our daughters gasped and covered their mouths. I began to protest to my wife that we did not have to eat it. We could order something else as the man stood over me waiting for my wife to finish her sentence. She said, "What's the matter, honey?" I knew I had to confess. I did not want to put that thing in my mouth! So, I told her honestly, "If you eat it then I have to eat it." As she put another huge bite in her mouth she said, "Then don't eat it." I said, "I cannot go back to the states and tell people you ate it and I did not have the courage to do it." She giggled, and said, "You really have a problem." Then she put another bite in her mouth.

After a big gulp she said something really strange. "Try it honey, it tastes really good!" So, I looked up at the waiter like a man who had lost the World Cup, and said, "Va benni, okay." He laid it there and said something about how I would never regret it and ran back to the kitchen, probably to get some more. I could not look at it as I cut into my first bite. It made a squishy sound that did not help and I put it into my mouth. It seemed like forever as all three pair of eyes watched me.

I could not believe it! It tasted fantastic! The flavors were indescribable and it was really quite good. We laughed as my wife and I looked at each other with black ink around our mouths because we could not look at what we were eating. Our brains would begin to revolt. There was joy again around our table as our daughters kept saying they could not believe what they were seeing. We ate every bite.

As we were all sitting at home and laughing around our dining room table telling Rosa this story she really laughed until I said that "my dream had momentarily turned into a nightmare." The laughing stopped and we knew something was wrong. As we began asking her questions and listened intently to what she was saying we would discover that this beautiful, petite, southern Italian woman of 27 years stopped taking afternoon naps (something that is really sacred in Puglia, the region where we lived) over 20 years ago because she has intense horrifying nightmares each and every time she goes to sleep.

So, since she did not want to experience two nightmares in a 24-hour period, she stayed awake while the rest of the city napped. Something welled up in my heart and I reached across the table and took her hand as my wife and daughters came close to embrace her and I said, "Could we pray and ask God to rid you of these nightmares?" She was stunned, and before she could think, tears welled up in her eyes and she nodded a "Yes."

We bowed our heads and prayed this simple prayer. "God, You are the Giver of dreams, and the Killer of nightmares. Would you please touch Rosa and completely deliver her from these tormenting nightmares and restore peaceful comforting dreams to her life? Would you come to her in her sleep and touch her heart and her mind and reveal your love, mercy and power to her in Jesus' name." We had never prayed with Rosa before. We all gave her the traditional kisses and a quick hug and said our goodbyes and out the door she went. I just stood at the door as she stepped into our small four-person elevator and wondered what God was going to do.

Many years ago not too far away from our new home there was a young man who had a night dream that he knew came from God, a God-dream, that had turned into a real life nightmare. He was a very normal teenager with a loving father who also had great God-dreams stored inside his heart. He had started his day like any other when his dad asked him to run an errand and check on his brothers working in another part of the countryside. His name was Joseph, son of Jacob. He had eleven brothers and one sister, some of whom were struggling in their relationship with their father and their life direction. Here is what happened to Joseph when he went to meet with them:

"When they saw him from a distance and before he came close to them, they plotted against him to put him to death.

And they said to one another, "Here comes this dreamer! Now then, come and let us kill him and throw him into one of the pits; and we will say, 'A wild beast devoured him.' Then let us see what will become of his dreams!"

Genesis 37:18–20 (NASB)

I have three main heroes of the Bible, other than Jesus, that I cannot seem to get away from as I read this sacred book over and over: Joseph, the natural father of Jesus, Jonathan, the close friend and legitimate heir to the throne of Saul of which King David took possession of and Joseph, the son of Jacob. I guess it is because I could see the reality of their lives and how they lived their lives against the backdrop of real human drama and yet were able to embrace the dream that God gave them which was deeply woven into the fabric of their lives. Joseph was indeed a dreamer. His brothers got that right. And the dreams he had been entrusted with were from no other source than God Himself.

Yet, today, many in the Kingdom of God confuse "God-dreams" with fantasy and "true destiny" with powerless hope. I have been pondering this issue for some time now and have had the privilege to share my "dreamy" thoughts with respected spiritual fathers and mothers around the world and discovered that this concept is deeply rooted in the Bible and I believe in the spiritual DNA of every living soul on the face of the earth.

God is the Giver of dreams and the Killer of nightmares. Not just night dreams but authentic God-dreams. How do I know that? Rosa taught me that. Two days after that gentle conversation in our apartment, she called us with an unspeakable joy in her voice. My whole family gathered around the receiver as I motioned to them that it was Rosa on the other end of the line. She said, "I have not had a nightmare since you prayed with me!" We are still in touch with her to this day. She is married and has a beautiful child of her own now and her testimony is that God destroyed those nightmares for her.

And His promise is for you as well. He is the Giver of dreams and Killer of nightmares. This book is not about night dreams even though God has and does still speak to people through them. This book is about God-dreams. God-dreams are those untapped visions, ideas and plans that God has placed inside of you for your life to have direction and substance. The God-dreams are in your heart and mind for a purpose. They are the road map that leads you to your destiny. We all have heard and believe that we have a purpose and destiny but many of us must admit that we are not sure how to get to the place of fulfilling the very destiny the Bible teaches us that we have. You were created for a reason. Yes, even if you are living a real nightmare right now, God wants to do for you what He did for Rosa and her sleeping night-mares, for Joseph and for me and countless others. He wants to unleash you into the God-dream that He has woven into your heart that will serve you until your last dying breath and will be a faithful friend until the end.

The enemy of your soul does not want you to get in touch with this truth because he knows if you do, nothing will stop you from connecting with other "dreamers" and starting a dream releasing revolution all over the world! I invite you to come with me on this journey. I think your heart is already telling you that it will be worth the time invested.

Chapter One

The DreamWeaver

There is nothing like *a dream* to create the future.

—Victor Hugo

For Thou didst form my inward parts;

Thou didst *weave me* in my mother's womb.

I will give thanks to Thee, for I am fearfully

and wonderfully made;

wonderful are Thy works, and my soul knows it very well.

My frame was not hidden from Thee,

when I was made in secret,

and *skillfully wrought* in the depths of the earth.

—Psalm 139:13–14 (NASB)

I was standing on the platform of one of the largest congregations in Mexico. I was in Puebla, Mexico to be exact. I was about to share the story of Joseph with the audience like I had done in so many different cities around the world when the Holy Spirit dropped this new thought into my heart. "Tell them that I have another name! My name is not only Jehovah Jireh, Jehovah Rophe but also . . .

"The DreamWeaver!"

I knew where God was going. We had discussed this earlier in the day. Psalm 139:13 (NASB) says, *"For Thou didst form my inward parts; Thou didst **weave me** in my mother's womb."* Yes, God created us physically and masterfully took the DNA strands from our parents, their parents and so on to make us into who we are today. Like a master painter, sculptor or architect, He sees His creation BEFORE it is ever created! He saw each of us and His plan for our lives BEFORE we took shape. It doesn't stop there! He also wove into us a destiny and "*the map*" that would lead us on this adventure that is as real and unique as the nose on your face. I call them "God-dreams." What happens when a God-dream is smothered, stolen or even lost? As a young man I was pondering this question and asking God to reveal this answer to me. I was expecting something like a lightning bolt kind of response but the answer came in a way I wasn't expecting. The answer came packaged in the life of a 70-year old man.

It was just an average day. I had been asked by my pastor to speak that Sunday morning on "sharing the hope that was within you" outside the four walls of the church building and really outside our comfort zones. I do not remember the exact text or even what I said but I do remember Martin. Martin was a short, elderly and very quiet man. He never said much and when he did it was so quiet you had to lean in closer just to hear him. Many times you had to ask him to repeat his words. Yet, he had a heart of gold and would willingly give you the "shirt off his back" if he thought you needed it. He owned a small country store in a small country town. One time he heard about a team from our church going to serve an orphanage in a faraway land, and before anyone knew it he had provided over seventy pair of shoes for the children in need. Not used—they were all brand new.

That Sunday morning as we were closing the service I asked if anyone wanted to make a new commitment to God, to make themselves available to go outside of their comfort zones to share the hope that was within them and trust God to guide them to the next step. No one came forward. The music began to play and still no one responded. Then I noticed someone beginning to move. It was Martin. Martin just walked up the aisle step by step until he was at the prayer bench. By the time he knelt down to pray with someone he was sobbing. It was not one of those gentle public sobs. No, this was a gusher and he was weeping so loud everyone noticed. I made my way down to him and by the time I met him at the bench others began coming. All I remember then was that as I glanced down to my right side was that it was full of people praying with other people. I was totally focused on Martin. "What's wrong?" I asked as I knelt down in front of him. He could not answer because he was crying so hard. It was all he could do to breathe and let out the emotions that I would discover later had been bottled up inside of him for almost 53 years.

Finally, he caught his breath enough to speak. He told me that when he was a teenager, about the age of Joseph, he had a dream to be a servant of God overseas somewhere. He did not know where exactly but he knew that God had spoken to him clearly. So, I asked him for more information. He went on to explain that in his excitement he went to his pastor but before he could finish explaining what had happened the pastor shut him down and told him that he was not fit to serve in that way and it would never happen. And that was that. Fast forward 53 years and the untapped dreams were still there inside his heart crying out to be released. There was sorrow, regret and guilt for not doing what he believed God had called him to do for 53 long years.

Martin was crying not only for that but also because he believed it was too late for him to fulfill the dream God had placed in his heart. Now, I was the one crying. He was stunned and took out his hanky to blow his nose and looked in shock at the tears running down my face. I began to pray and ask God for forgiveness for all the "Martins" who had their dreams crushed by another person's interference. I stood in the place of this nameless pastor and asked God to forgive "me" for this sin and I asked Martin for forgiveness too. He did not know what to say. All I know is something powerful happened in this man's heart that morning. Something happened to me as well.

Like a lightning bolt this thought came into my mind. In about six months I was taking a team to serve the poor in Leogane, Haiti and I invited Martin to come. At first, he began to give me all of the reasons that he could think of why it could not happen: "I'm too old, I do not have that kind of money, I have nothing to offer this team." You know, things like that. Things we say to God when He uses someone or something to nudge us into the path of our God-dream. After he exhausted all the excuses we went to work. Martin did not even write letters to raise his support like most people do.

The word got out and the money came rolling in. Martin was going to Haiti to serve God! So, much money came in we had to tell people to stop giving because his need was met and so were his teammates'.

That summer, Martin went to Haiti and helped us put a roof on some mission buildings, feed poor children and do church programs. I still have an old wrinkled photo of Martin standing by a river with seven naked Haitian children hanging all over him. They were there swimming and they had struck up a friendship and wanted a photo together. Every time I look at it and remember what happened that

Sunday morning my heart swells with the light of God's goodness.

To my knowledge Martin never went back to Haiti or any other country for that matter. But he was never the same after that and neither was I. I had witnessed the power of seeing a God-dream released. Even a dream like Martin's that had been smothered by the reckless words of someone else for years. I believe that the dream that God has woven within each and every human being is crying out to be released. Everywhere I go now I see this truth being confirmed whether it is a movie, a story that someone shares at a coffee shop or even in the most unlikely places like an old song.

It was a muggy and really sweltering evening. I was walking on the streets in Hoi On, just a few kilometers away from the city of Danang, Vietnam. We were there on a "humanitarian trip" as a medical team. This was our last night and I wanted to pick up something for my wife to celebrate our upcoming anniversary. It was kind of a personal ritual of mine.

Every year I was usually somewhere in the world sharing the love of Christ and I would look for something different and unique for my wife to celebrate our anniversary. This trip was no different because I was a man on a mission. I did not know what I wanted but when I found it I would know it. I wandered into a shop displaying some unusual artwork. At first I thought they were oil paintings. I was wrong. Every piece was done free hand by a local artist. The images were scenes captured from an Asian setting. There were boats, houses, people, rice fields and even bouquets of flowers. They looked like someone had painted them with beautiful oil but they were entirely made from *threads*. They were made entirely from silk thread to be exact.

The manager of the shop was so proud of what they were doing I was invited to the second floor to see the actual silk worms actively engaging their trade! I was amazed. After two and a half to three sweaty hours of going back and forth into this shop, we agreed on a price and they rolled up my gift for Bev and I tucked it into my backpack like a hunter who captured his prey on an African safari!

Later that night inside my room, I wanted to take a look at the prize I had just "bagged." When I opened the piece of art I opened it face down so as not to soil it in any way with my sweaty fingers. When fully opened, the masterpiece I had pictured in my mind was a mess! There were thousands of threads in all kinds of colors but they were in knots like the remains of hurricane after the storm on a small Caribbean island! I could not believe what I was seeing. Then I turned it over; there it was—a beautiful masterpiece!

A three dimensional piece of art with thread that revealed texture, color, shadows and every detail one would want in a masterpiece. Even the cloth that was used to house this masterpiece was a woven piece of silk. As I kept flipping the image over and over, back and forth on my bed looking at the contrast of the two sides of the image, God spoke this to my heart, "This is a great illustration of my Word over your life when I 'wove you together in your mother's womb.' Many times you look at your life from the *back side* instead of the side that I am looking at—*the finished side*."

That is so true not only of my life but the way many today look at their lives. Maybe you do it as well. You know what we tend to do; we focus on the knots, the mess, mistakes and the nightmares. And we are totally distracted from the God-dream. We never take the time to look at our lives from God's perspective and "flip the picture over." We need to spend time with God cultivating our comfort with His presence as well as His Word to do the accurate "flipping." We need time alone with God to get another perspective—His perspective, which is so important.

When I talked with the manager of this small store in Vietnam she filled in all the details of what went into making this masterpiece I would eventually give to my bride. One woman spent eight to ten hours a day for eight weeks with just her own two hands crafting this image. She wove the threads of many different colors knowing exactly what she was doing and in her mind what the finished product would look like.

God is like that. He knows the number of hairs (and the lack thereof) on our heads, the end from the beginning and even where we will live most of our lives (Acts 17:26). He has woven into the core of our very lives God-dreams that will guide us to the destiny that He has for us to give us a hope and a future! (Jeremiah 29:11). My friend and mentor, Wayne Cordeiro says, "*A dream without faith is fantasy.*" That is so true. This is the reason that before you can run with the God-dream in your heart you must really *believe* in it yourself. You must live from God's perspective not yours. Your perspective and mine are so limited. But God's is so incredibly vast. He does know the end from the beginning. This is why Joseph could say to his brothers after approximately 20 years in slavery and prison these very words:

"I am Joseph! Is my father still alive?" But his brothers could not answer him, for they were dismayed at his presence. Then Joseph said to his brothers, "Please come closer to me." And they came closer. And he said, "I am your brother Joseph, whom you sold into Egypt. "And now do not be grieved or angry with yourselves, because you sold

*me here; **for God sent me before you to preserve life**. "For the famine has been in the land these two years, and there are still five years in which there will be neither plowing nor harvesting. "And God sent me before you to preserve for you a remnant in the earth, and to keep you alive by **a great deliverance**. "Now, therefore, it was not you who sent me here, **but God**; and He has made me **a father** to Pharaoh and lord of all his household and ruler over all the land of Egypt.* Genesis 45:3–8 (NASB)

Joseph had a dream that he was living but had endured a nightmare at the hands of his brothers and yet his perspective that I believe he *stole* from God—was clear with two powerful words: "*But God!*" I am not sure what is happening in your life today regarding the God-dream He has woven into your life but I am convinced that if we follow Joseph's example and cling to God's perspective we will see things from a totally different vantage point and can live, respond and function in a new framework that most people do not see or understand. Unfortunately, people do not follow Joseph's path. Let me give you just one of many possible examples.

Joseph walked with God and had received His perspective. His brothers would not be so fortunate. They would carry a limited perspective for many years. After this Joseph was a blessing to them and their families but they would not accept it. They would hold their limited perspective in their hearts until the day their father Jacob would die. And after his death and burial their perspective would reveal itself:

*When Joseph's brothers saw that their father was dead, they said, "What if Joseph should bear a grudge against us and pay us back in full for all the wrong which we did to him!" So they sent a message to Joseph, saying, "Your father charged before he died, saying, 'Thus you shall say to Joseph, "Please forgive, I beg you, the transgression of your brothers and their sin, for they did you wrong. And now, please forgive the transgression of the servants of the God of your father.'" And Joseph wept when they spoke to him. Then his brothers also came and fell down before him and said, "Behold, we are your servants." But Joseph said to them, "Do not be afraid, for am I in God's place? "And as for you, you meant evil against me, **but God** meant it for good in order to bring about this present result, to preserve many people alive. "So therefore, do not be afraid; I will provide for you and your little ones." So he comforted them and spoke kindly to them.*

Genesis 50:15–21 (NASB)

One day I was talking to a very close friend about what happened to me in Mexico and that I had discovered a new name of God in the Bible found in Psalm 139:13-15. When I told him that was going to be the name of this book and as we talked about those verses he reminded me about a song that was very popular in the 1970's with the same title: "Dream Weaver!" I faintly remembered that song from my teen years. So, I did some research to discover some amazing details that I never knew before. Here are the words to jog your memory . . .

I have just closed my eyes again
Climbed aboard the Dream Weaver train
Driver take away my worries of today
And leave tomorrow behind . . .
Dream Weaver . . . I believe you can get me through
the night
Dream Weaver . . . I believe we can reach the morning light
Fly me through the starry skies
Or maybe to an astral plane
Cross the highways of fantasy
Help me to forget today's pain
Dream Weaver... I believe you can get me through the night
Dream Weaver... I believe we can reach the morning light

Though the dawn may be coming soon
There still may be some time
Fly me away to the bright side of the moon
And meet me on the other side
Dream Weaver . . . I believe you can get me through
the night
Dream Weaver . . . I believe we can reach the morning light

Gary Wright, the author of this popular song said that "'Dream Weaver, I believe you can get me through the night' was a song about Someone with infinite compassion and love carrying us through the night of our trials and suffering. *None other than God Himself.*" Wow! I found that interesting for a man who does not claim to be a follower of Jesus.

For some this will have no meaning whatsoever, but I look for the truth of God everywhere because that is where He is! In verse 15 of Psalm 139 there is another clue: "*My frame was not hidden from Thee, when I was made in secret, and skillfully wrought in the depths of the earth.*" The words "*skillfully wrought*" literally mean: "to *variegate* color, i.e. *embroider*; by implication to *fabricate*; embroiderer, needle-work, curiously work."

When I stumble onto clues like this lights start going off in my head like the old blue light special at Kmart! For example, many people look at Joseph, son of Jacob as some kind of spoiled child who probably deserved the treatment he received from his family concerning his "lofty dreams."

I see something totally different. Take his "varicolored tunic" given to him by his father. Was it just to spoil him? Or did it mean something totally different to Joseph, his father and most of all his brothers? Have we missed something when we read the text in Genesis superficially? Is God trying to tell us something about His Weaving in our lives? Is there more to the Joseph story than we already know? It is the answer to these kinds of questions I want to ponder with you next.

Chapter Two

Book With Your Name

"You may say I'm a dreamer,

but *I'm not the only one*,

I hope someday you will join us,

and the world will live as one."

—John Lennon

"You saw me *before* I was born.

Every day of my life was *recorded in your book.*

Every moment was *laid out before a single day*

had passed."

—Psalm 139:16 (NLT)

It was February, 1958. On a cold winter day in Muncie, Indiana there was a family in turmoil—mine. My parents had a broken marriage and the final straw that broke the proverbial camel's back was *centered around* me. I was still in my mother's womb when the final blow came but basically my mother left a man, my biological father, who struggled with his character to the point that she believed my life and hers would be in danger if we stayed with him. I love my mom for that. So she moved home with her parents, Belmer and Alice Johnson. I called them Grandpa and Grandma Johnson. My grandfather was a fiery Baptist preacher who died when I was only ten years old. I never knew why but out of eight children and 42 grandchildren (at last count) I had a very special relationship with my Grandma Johnson that would last until she passed away. There was just something about her that still deeply warms my heart when I think of her. She too has recently gone to be with her Lord and Savior but before she would leave this earth she would make an eternal impact on my life which I believe was designed by none other than God Himself.

My mom was living with her parents and my grandmother told me eighteen years later when I had committed my life to follow Christ that she was not surprised at the radical events taking place in my life at that time. I had made a lot of mistakes up to that point so I was very curious about her insights. She told me many stories but one made an imprint in my heart that I will never forget. She said I was only a few days old and I had come home from the hospital and she was rocking me in front of the big glass window on Macedonia Avenue in Muncie, Indiana. It was raining and cold and the wind was blowing. She began to sing over me, but sing as she did her heart was anxious for this little boy and his future.

As she sang tears began to flow so steady down her face that they were dropping on my little chubby arms and face and as she was wiping them off the Lord spoke this promise to her heart that she would never forget. Nor will I. The Lord said, "Your tears of sorrow today have become an "oil of anointing" for my servant Sammy Ray. He will not only grow up and find me but he will give his heart to me and I will use him to speak hope to nations all over the world." When she told me this I was stunned. I had only known the Lord for a very short time and was just beginning to read my Bible. But every time I would visit her she would check in to see where I was on my "promised journey" with God. She knew I would preach and she knew I would do it all over the world. How could she know that? I did not know it. But every time we spoke something stirred inside of me. And I began to piece seemingly insignificant events together that started to feel like *pages of a book*. An early morning encounter with God where I thought I heard something to the effect I would have a strong ministry in Spain. Spain? What is that all about? Then there were these events with foreign nationals who would come to our country and every time I was with them I felt a comfort, connection and even, yes, a kinship unlike anything I could describe or put into words. Was this just random unrelated incidents or was there something else going on?

Something was *awakened* inside of me. I began to ask God if this was true. Before my grandmother died I did receive a call to preach and did preach in her small Baptist church in Florida. It would be many years later that the rest of that prophetic promise would come true. At this writing

I have now been to over 90 countries and preached in most of them. "How" did she know? I would ask this many times. But the Lord finally spoke to me one day and said, "You are asking the wrong question. It's not 'how' but 'Who?'"

The Psalmist writes, "*You saw me before I was born. Every day of my life was recorded in your book. Every moment was laid out before a single day had passed.*" Just think about that for a moment. *Every moment of every day was recorded in a book with your name on it*! I know that this is an easy thing to say or write but to really believe it to the point that you make life decisions based on that belief is entirely something else.

When I was first confronted with this truth I could not even accept the fact that God had given me the name I had. I used to say to myself: "My name is *Sammy Ray Scaggs*? Why do I have such a "sissy name" like that? Why couldn't it have at least been a name like Chuck, Michael, or even Joseph, something that had a masculine ring to it? Sammy Ray? Come on God! You mean that you knew this and did nothing about it?" I even went to great lengths to disguise it. I would never tell anyone what my legal name was. I would let them think it was Samuel. Or I would put on my bank checks "Sam R. Scaggs." But it would just gnaw on me as not being authentic.

One day as I was doing a study on the topic that God has chosen each and every one of us for a purpose I ran across passage after passage where God was involved in the naming process of individuals. In some cases God would actually tell the parents what to name their children as in the cases of Ishmael and Isaac.

The Old Testament prophet Isaiah takes it a step further and says,

Listen to me, all you in distant lands! Pay attention, you who are far away!

*The Lord called me before my birth; from within the womb **he called me by name**.* (Isaiah 49:1) (NLT)

Jeremiah says,

*The Lord gave me this message: "I knew you before I formed you in your mother's womb. **Before you were born I set you apart and appointed you** as my prophet to the nations."* (Jeremiah 1:4–5) (NLT)

I remember bowing my head and telling the Lord that I was getting it. Just the fact that I was struggling with my name had more to reveal to me than I was even aware of—I was struggling with my identity, my direction, my destiny and ultimately my God-dream. I repented that day and embraced my full name as it is and something changed inside of me from that time forward. Something was *set in order.*

When Joseph began to come to a realization that his life was more than what he had imagined and more complicated, he knew it was connected to his identity. The Bible reveals that Joseph was given a "varicolored tunic" or what some call the "coat of many colors." A superficial look at his life will give you the impression that it was a gift of favoritism. I disagree with that conclusion completely. I believe the coat of many colors has a multifaceted message for us today. I believe it first of all it symbolized the decision his father had made regarding who was in succession to lead his family once he was gone.

You see, Joseph, like many in our world today was caught up in some events that he had no control over—even his dysfunctional family life. His father had two wives who were sisters (Leah and Rachel). Leah gave birth to four sons; Reuben, Simeon, Levi and Judah as well as one daughter, Dinah. Joseph's mother was Rachel who made him the firstborn in that relationship and later he would have only one full-blooded brother, Benjamin. And in the competition for children each of his wives gave Jacob their servant girls (Zilpah and Bilhah) to bear even more children (Gad, Asher, Dan & Naphtali). All in all there were twelve sons who would eventually form the twelve tribes of the nation of Israel. But for Joseph it would create enough drama to last his entire life!

In the days of Joseph it was simple to determine who would succeed the father and lead the tribe once he had passed away. The firstborn was that person. But since Jacob had four wives (two he married and two who were given as two concubines or common-law wives, Zilpah and Bilhah) there was some confusion to say the least. Technically speaking Reuben, born to Leah should have been the rightful heir but he was disqualified because he slept with his father's concubine, Bilhah and that would end it for Jacob. Then there was the conspiracy that Reuben's brothers, Simeon and Levi, would be involved in avenging their sister, Dinah's rape and would bring shame and reproach to Jacob and their family. The bottom line is that the first three sons from Leah were not qualified to lead the tribe of Jacob and *everyone* knew this.

It was obvious to *everyone* that Joseph not only was the rightful heir but the one with the character and fortitude to assume that responsibility. But just because it is the right thing to do does not always make it acceptable to everyone involved. I am sure you have either experienced this or at the very least seen it happen to someone around you. This was the case for Joseph. With that background look carefully at the simple words recorded in Genesis about what happened:

Joseph, when seventeen years of age, was pasturing the flock with his brothers while he was still a youth, along with the sons of Bilhah and the sons of Zilpah, his father's wives. And Joseph brought back a bad report about them to their father. Now Israel loved Joseph more than all his sons, because he was the son of his old age; and he made him a varicolored tunic. And his brothers saw that their father loved him more than all his brothers; and so they hated him and could not speak to him on friendly terms. Then Joseph had a dream, and when he told it to his brothers, they hated him even more. And he said to them, "Please listen to this dream which I have had; for behold, we were binding sheaves in the field, and lo, my sheaf rose up and also stood erect; and behold, your sheaves gathered around and bowed down to my sheaf." Then his brothers said to him, "Are you actually going to reign over us? Or are you really going to rule over us?" So they hated him even more for his dreams and for his words. Now he had still another dream, and related it to his brothers, and said, "Lo, I have had still another dream;

and behold, the sun and the moon and eleven stars were bowing down to me." And he related it to his father and to his brothers; and his father rebuked him and said to him, "What is this dream that you have had? Shall I and your mother and your brothers actually come to bow ourselves down before you to the ground?" And his brothers were jealous of him, but his father kept the saying in mind.

Genesis 37:2–11 (NASB)

It is my conclusion that Joseph was not being arrogant. He was being honest. Honesty was not a high priority then and it still isn't today, even in the Church at large when it comes to God-dreams. We struggle with speaking the truth in love. We struggle with hearing the truth. We struggle with living the truth. Some of it is because we have seen how people react when truth is encountered. We have heard and read about people who stand up for truth and we wonder if we want to pay that kind of price! Joseph was sharing a dream that I am sure he did not totally understand at age seventeen. His dream, which happened to be a God-dream, was beyond the dream that even his own father had for his life. It was huge! It was a big audacious and hairy dream! The kind of dream that is either so big that it must be from

God or at the very least someone who has a great imagination. Just bear with me for a moment.

That is the trouble we have with authentic God-dreams. They are usually so big we think it is our imagination. And if we become bold enough to share ours with someone else we are met with unbelief, jealousy and sometimes even anger or resentment. So, we just stuff it.

We keep the dream undercover but over time it begins to seep out. We slip and we just go ahead and confide in someone to see what their reaction will be. Just like Martin did when he shared his dream with his pastor at an early age and it was snuffed out. Just like Joseph did and the entire family was upset with him. What was it like that night when Joseph lay down in his tent with the voices of anger and unbelief that he could still hear ringing in his ears? Did he shrug it off and go to sleep? Or did he look out the tent flap and into the sky and say, "I believe my God-dream?" Did he play with the fabric of his coat of many colors, rubbing the soft and fine fibers between his fingers and say to himself, "God, *just as my father wove this tunic from many colorful threads together and made it into something beautiful to wear, are You weaving even these difficult things into my life for a purpose?*"

You see, the truth is, you have been chosen for a purpose. Your life does have meaning and God does have a plan for you. The plan is so detailed that He wrote everything, every moment of every day, down in a book and put your name on it! Imagine, God's incredible library with billions of books alphabetically in order. One for each and every person ever conceived yesterday, today and tomorrow. And there it is; your book with your name on the spine! It is sticking out and ready to be pulled down and read. Do you see it? Aren't you just a little bit curious what He wrote about you? Don't you want to just reach out and grab it and look at the inside flap or the table of contents, read just a few pages, flip ahead to the last chapter to see what is going to happen? I do!

This is what your God-dream is all about. It is not daydreaming we are talking about. It is not fantasy, mythology, or just another crazy idea somebody cooked up. This is your life! When you say "Yes" to God and His plan for your life and have the courage to walk down the path and step out in faith to experience the dream He has for you it is like pulling that book with your name on it off the shelf and taking a peek inside!

There are some other clues that will help you in this discovery and they are not as difficult as you might think to find them. Let's continue this journey together and discover what they might be.

Chapter Three

Who's Your Daddy?

Some men see things as they are and say, "Why?"
I dream of things that never were and say, "Why not?"
—George Bernard Shaw

"There are a lot of people around who can't
wait to tell you what you've done wrong,
but there aren't many fathers willing to
take the time and effort to help you
grow up. It was as Jesus helped me
proclaim God's Message to you
that I became your father."
—The Apostle Paul, 1 Corinthians 4:15 (MSG)

I am a movie buff. There, I said it. I think that stories are an incredible medium to communicate truth, emotion and restore the ability to imagine the things God-dreams are made of. I also believe that there are many conspiracies out there that the enemy of our souls wants to use to limit or destroy our imagination. Jesus was the Master Story Teller. If He was here today I think he would produce incredible movies! So, movies, like any medium can be used for good or evil. I love the good ones.

There is an incredible story, based on actual events, portrayed in the feature film entitled *"Remember the Titans."* As the story goes, an African-American football coach was hired at an all-white high school in Alexandria, Virginia in the mid 1960's, to be the head coach just when racial tensions were running high due to forced integration of public schools.

To complicate matters further, the current coach, who was white, was given the choice to either leave or be made his assistant coach.

Needless to say, that the possibility of this story turning out with a positive ending was next to nil. That is why it became a major motion picture, because the people were transformed, the school was transformed and the entire community was transformed as well. In one particular scene Coach Boone raises a question of "order" with Gary and his friend to reveal that a new reality has just come into play with his leadership of the football team. He asks Gary: *"Who's your daddy?"*

It was a fair question that changes the entire direction of the story. He goes on to point out to Gary and everyone else on the team both black and white in this season, the fall football season, he was their "daddy" and the rest of the team members are his "brothers." In other words, there is going to be a "new order" and with that order life is going to be totally different. Coach Boone was tough but it would take "tough love" in order to do what he was sent there to do. Another "coach" who fits the description of "tough love" is the Apostle Paul.

"Coach Paul" said something powerful to a group of people in a similar situation to Coach Boone's team,

"For even if you had ten thousand others
to teach you about Christ,
you have only one spiritual father.
For I became your father in
Christ Jesus when I preached the Good News to you."
1 Corinthians 4:15 (NLT)

Let's read it again from the Message Version:
"There are a lot of people around who can't wait to tell
you what you've done wrong, but there aren't many fathers
willing to take the time and effort to help you grow up. It
was as Jesus helped me proclaim God's Message to you
that I became your father."
1 Corinthians 4:15 (MSG)

What was Paul talking about? What caused him to say such a thing? Paul knew the Scriptures well and he knew that the church age had come and something powerful needed to happen to bring this thing to a climax. Malachi 4:5-6 (NLT) explains,

"See, I will send you the prophet Elijah before that great
and dreadful day of the Lord comes. He will turn the
hearts of the fathers to their children, and the hearts of the

children to their fathers; or else I will come and strike the land with a curse."

In other words, God is going to intentionally reestablish a new order of father and son so that things that have run amuck in the lives of people can be set on the right path again. I truly believe that God's intended order is for birth parents to raise their natural children to seek and know God the Father with their whole hearts. Then as they grow and develop those skills, they will encounter people in their daily lives who have been orphaned not only in the physical sense but in the spiritual sense as well and will take them into the spheres of their family to be nurtured when others have abandoned them.

There are many people in the world and in our local congregations who have this "orphan spirit" active in their lives and they are walking with God but they are confused about their identity, about their destiny and the dream that God has placed within their heart is all locked up begging to be released! Spiritual fathers and mothers can be used of God to help unleash men and women and watch them embrace their God-dreams and their God-given destinies no matter what has happened in their past. This is the kind of God we serve!

For many of us today there is a major gap in our understanding of what Malachi prophesied and what Paul says has happened as a result of Christ and the work He did on Calvary. It was Dr. Mark Handby who opened my eyes to this truth and helped me answer these kinds of questions in his book, "You Have Not Many Fathers." Why did Malachi proclaim that a man would come in the same spirit as the prophet Elijah? Why not Moses, Joseph, King David, Jeremiah, or even Isaiah? The Gospel of Luke gives us a clue. In Luke chapter 1, the Angel Gabriel is speaking to the father of John the Baptist and foretells of his ministry . . .

*He will be a man **with** the spirit and power of Elijah,*
the prophet of old.
He will precede the coming of the Lord,
preparing the people for his
arrival. He will turn the hearts of the fathers
to their children, and
he will change disobedient minds to accept godly wisdom.
—Luke 1:17 (NLT)

The coming of Jesus would turn the world upside down and inside out! Not only did His coming provide us with forgiveness and access to the Father Heart of God, but it would forever change how we relate to one another! God would put His heart in each one of us and, as we mature, we would become His hands and feet, mouth and eyes, words and touch in this decaying world! The Apostle Paul admonished a young preacher by the name of Timothy to:

> *"Never speak harshly to an older man, but appeal to him*
> *respectfully as though he*
> *were your own father. Talk to the younger men*
> *as you would to your own*
> *brothers. Treat the older women as you would*
> *your mother, and treat the*
> *younger women with all purity as your own sisters."*
> —1 Timothy 5:1–2 (NLT)

This was not some superficial command to make people get along in the church. Everything changes when you enter the Kingdom of God. There is a *new order*! Those who were once strangers are now family and those who had no one now have a family that encompasses the entire world!

God has adopted you into His family and He IS YOUR HEAVENLY FATHER because He has *always* loved you. He has provided a way for you to receive what He intended for you just as if you had been born into a Godly family. His perfect plan was for your natural parents to fulfill the role of Godly covering, but if that is thwarted, God will fulfill His purposes through someone else. With a spiritual father and mother, God can still fulfill that plan. His purpose for you will prevail.

"Who's Your Daddy?" is a fantastic question because God has prepared someone to fulfill that role for each of us. And one of His primary purposes is to create a safe place for the God-dream to emerge! It is awesome for the spiritual fathers and mothers to be a conduit of God the Father and it is awesome for spiritual sons and daughters to be recipients of this grace! Everyone wins when God's order is set into place.

This is the key issue between Jacob and all thirteen of his children. Especially between the sons of his two wives, Leah and Rachael; this puts Joseph at odds with Reuben and the other brothers. Even though it is another time and culture and today it is not acceptable to have more than one wife, there is still much dysfunction between families with skyrocketing divorce rates, remarriage, unfaithfulness and all the children who have been estranged by one or both of their parents or are put in the middle of the strained relationships of their parents. All of this has an effect on people, their relation-ship with God as their Heavenly Father, their identities, their

God-dreams and ultimately their destiny in the one and only life they will have.

I feel rather passionate about all of this because I like many others have not only experienced the challenge as a child but now have my own children and have experienced this tension within my own extended family. There is no question that there is enough pressure on families today to go around. I have been married over three decades to an incredible woman. She should just get a medal for being married to me. I am not walk in the park. But her faithfulness and perseverance and dedication to me and our children are something I cannot put into words.

We have had the privilege of bringing three daughters into this world. Our first daughter Audrey Faith died the day she was born and it was a day of disappointment, sorrow and pain I never imagined. God was faithful and so were our family and brothers and sisters in Christ who walked with us through that nightmare.

Then exactly one year later we were blessed with Rebekah Joy. Her name reflected her destiny with us. A beautiful person inside and out who has and continues to bring us much joy.

Sarah Denise is our third and she too lives up to her name, which means "princess." She is a daughter of a King and His name is Jesus. Our daughters have grown into two beautiful young women who love Jesus and are serving Him today. Our life as a family has not been perfect to say the least. But we are blessed for sure and we give God all the praise for His love, grace and mercy that has brought us to this point.

Everything that I am sharing with you has been thoroughly tested. Our daughter Rebekah went through a season in her life where she got off the path that we had dreamed for her to walk on. And yes, I asked for her permission to share this with you. It is so pivotal to this message in my heart it cannot be left out. A long story short, she experienced the pain of divorce and then later giving birth to our first grandson, Ethan as an unwed mother. The enemy would try to use this difficult time to do three things. First, he would try to destroy our relationship as parents with her, something we refused to let happen. Second, he tried to destroy our daughter, something the enemy should never to do to parents when they love their children. And thirdly, he wanted to destroy our precious grandson. Man, don't mess with a someone's grandchild— you are starting a fight that will be fought to the death!

We were heartbroken as any parent would be during a season like this and many nights I cried into my pillow fighting all the thoughts of how I failed her as a father—both as a natural and as a spiritual father. God was so gentle with me during those tender days. He just kept whispering into my ear this simple but powerful word of advice, "Just continue to love her *the way* I love you!" How does God, the Father love you and me? What is this *"way?"* He loves us unconditionally. He loves us no matter what we do. He is always incredibly kind towards us. He loves us enough to tell us the truth even if it hurts. Yet He never stops loving us nor does He stop relating to us *the way* a true loving father does. He loves us like the father in the story of two sons in the gospel of Luke, chapter fifteen. Yes, it is a story that describes the love of God for us before we know Christ but it is also a great story to remind us of *how He loves us after we commit our lives to Christ.*

The day Ethan, our firstborn grandson was born was a day that I will never forget as long as I live. When we were in the hospital room and the contractions were just beginning my daughter looked into my eyes and said, "Oh Daddy, it hurts!" I did what any dad would do—I ran for cover! Her mom was on duty for this assignment and I knew my place was going to be in the prayer room until our grandchild arrived. I was so confused that day because I was a trooper when my wife gave birth to our three daughters. I went through Lamaze childbirth training and thought I was a great partner with my wife. But when our daughter looked into my eyes and I knew what was coming I knew I would not be the best one to help that day—her mom was that person.

Once the news came later that afternoon that Ethan was here, my wife came out to the waiting room crying. I was frightened. She was crying so hard that she could not communicate what was on her heart to us. So, I began to ask questions for one-word answers! "Is Becky okay? Is Ethan okay? Does he have all ten fingers and toes? The answer was "Yes!" to every question. "Then, what's wrong?" I asked. My wife managed to say through her tears, "He is so beautiful!" Less than two minutes later we were in the room and everyone was taking care of and congratulating my daughter and the nurse put Ethan in my arms for the very first time! It was my turn now. I began to cry. I love our daughters but this was the firstborn son in our family and something powerful began to happen in my heart.

As I watched the tears from my eyes fall on his little chubby arms I had a flashback to a story that my grandmother painted in my heart forty-five years earlier in Muncie, Indiana. And it all came together for me. My daughter and grandson were in the same kind of challenge that my mother and I were in and the Father Heart of God that had seen us through with my grandmother was now alive in my heart. I could choose to be a religious leader and judge my family or

I could be a *true father* and love my daughter and her first-born son unconditionally and trust God's kindness to draw them to back to Himself. That is exactly what my wife and I chose to do. I remember praying over my grandson in those brief moments and it was glorious.

I do not have it all figured out for sure but I do know one thing: it is the loving kindness of God that calls us out of darkness and into His marvelous light. It is His loving kindness that lights the pathway when we get lost and it is His loving kindness that covers, washes clean and removes a multitude of our sins.

Prior to these events God spoke through five servant leaders prophetically this word:

"Sam, the tears that you have shed in your pillow in the dark hours of night has not gone unnoticed. Do not be dismayed over the season of your oldest daughter. For not only will she return to Me but she will return to you as well and she will serve at your right hand in ministry."

These five leaders did not know each other, had never met my family and did not know about the others' spoken words. These words were spoken over a thirteen-month period and in five different locations of the world. By the time I received the fifth one in Spain from my now dear friend Cindy Jacobs, I told God, "Okay, I got your message!"

Today, our daughter is married to the father of my first-born grandson (and has given us a second grandson named Joel) and both have committed their lives to Christ and are members of a local church. Our daughter left the law firm where she was working as a paralegal and works as my Executive Assistant in our global coaching ministry! Does this sound like I am bragging? Yes, I am! I am bragging about y*our Heavenly Father* and mine. Who's your daddy? I hope you can say with me that God is truly your Father and that He has placed at least one spiritual father and/or mother in your life so your God-dream can be released into His Kingdom!

This is the first major clue to your God-dream! God will use your natural and/or spiritual fathers and mothers to help release the God-dream in your life. They will help create and cultivate an environment for this dream to be unleashed. They will bless and confirm upon you the dream that will lead you in the direction you need to go to embrace your God-given identity and destiny. They will be there for you when you go through the peaks and valleys to help you keep a God-perspective. And they will cheer you on when you feel like giving up! Do not underestimate the power of praying parents—both natural and/or spiritual. Do not give up on your parents. Do not give up on your children. Do not narrow your vision to just natural children as important as they are because God has plenty of people with the orphan spirit who need someone like you to model living the God-dream and to help their dream to be released. There are orphan churches but that is a topic for another day in another book!

Chapter Four

Here Comes this Dreamer

Trust in dreams. For in them is the *hidden gate to eternity*.

—Kahlil Gibran

"…So Joseph went after *his brothers* and found

them at Dothan. When they saw him from

a distance and before he came close to them,

they plotted against him to put him to death.

And they said to one another,

"*Here comes this dreamer*!

Now then, come and let us kill him

and throw him into one of the pits;

and we will say, 'A wild beast devoured him.'

Then let us see what will become of his dreams!"

—Genesis 37:17–20 (NASB)

I can honestly say that I did not choose the message of *"The DreamWeaver,"* it really chose me! I have always had a vivid imagination and I love a good story. Maybe that is one of the reasons that the story of Joseph, the son of Jacob has fascinated me so much. However, I am not one to be attracted to the dreams and visions and all of the mystical things that today's world and many others are so caught up in. I have not naturally been attracted to the nighttime sleeping dreams of Daniel, Nebuchadnezzar, or even Joseph, the husband of Mary. Yet, I have been totally captivated by the God-dreams that happened in the Bible and still happen today. When I talk with leaders around the world I find that they either love the whole "dream" topic (and usually it is more the mystical side of dreams), or they think it is foolish to even focus on the topic at all.

The latter equate dreams of any kind with fantasy. They put dreams in the "name it and claim it camp." You know, the philosophy that treats Jesus Christ and God like the Arabian fairy tale of Aladdin's Lamp, just "rub Him just the right way" and "poof," he appears and bows and says, "And what can I do for you today?" Sorry, I do not fit in any of those camps. I believe in the sovereign work of God and like the Apostle Paul many things continue to be a mystery. I believe in the power of the Holy Spirit to completely overwhelm us continually and releases our gifts, passion and dreams to lead us into our destiny to fulfill the purpose and mission He wove into the very fiber of our being while we were in our mother's womb.

Honestly, this is one of the reasons I have struggled with sharing the information in this book. If you do not fit in either of those camps then who is going to be interested in this message at all? I hope the rest of the world because I believe that there are billions of people and millions of followers of Jesus with a God-dream trapped inside of them and if we could just create a safe place within the Kingdom of God that would be a *"culture of honor"* and transparency *that is truly safe* and give people the *benefit of the doubt and believe the best about our brothers and sisters we would see more genuine miracles than we could ever imagine.* Not miracles that only some believe in but the kind of miracles that *everyone knows are from God*!

I know so many of the people who have taken the risk and stepped out of the "boat of safety" to follow their God-dreams like Joseph did by name and I could write (and maybe I will some day) an entire volume of their stories. But allow me to give you just a couple of examples. There are some very close friends of mine who is a doctor and spiritual parents to many. Dr. Chris and Nancy are a one of a kind couple. He is a very good doctor and yet, he had a dream that average men and women, young adults and teenagers could be recruited, trained and released to share the hope of the Gospel in places that CNN journalists do not like to go!

So, every year he does this. He, along with his wife, recruits and leads these teams of every day ordinary people to some of the most remote areas of the world to serve people who need medical care, encouragement and just someone to care and love them. And like clockwork, these folks want to know who they are and why they came and they tell them the story of the transforming power of Jesus! Not only do they tell them; they *show them by serving them and praying over them. They see so many people healed, touched and delivered it's absolutely amazing.* This is his God-dream! He is one of my God-dream heroes! I am keeping a list of them and the numbers are now in the hundreds!

Another example is their son, Sean and his wife Katie. His son and daughter-in-law have a passion for the nations (no surprise) and for the Body of Christ and wants so desperately to see the people of God set on fire for the things that burn in the heart of God so he and his wife decided to get together with some of their friends and seek God in worship and prayer non-stop for 12, 24, and 36 hours at a time. They simply call it the "Burn 24/7." It is *catching fire* (no pun intended) and spreading all over the USA and the world. I believe one day they will have a network of "Burn Centers" in every major city of the world! And this is not the end! This God-dream is not something they just thought up. It is something that has gripped them and they cannot sleep until they pursue it the way God has called them to do it.

I have just one more example to share with you. There are two women who are living their God-dream. They live in a restricted access nation that is among the coldest cities in the world! One of them is pediatric doctor and the other is a physical therapist. They left the cushy comforts of home and their successful medical practices and went to this country with nothing but a God-dream to touch the lives of these people any way they could. Today they have built a

"Dream Center" that is the home for an average of 30 babies under the age of three who have been left sometimes right on their doorstep, planted over seven congregations and they are serving in other areas of medical care where this city of thousands need modern health care. And if that is not enough, these single modern day female apostles have adopted between them four children of their own. They are my God-dream heroes! How do they do what they do? It cannot be explained except for the fact that God has placed a unique God-dream in them that will not diminish until they fulfill what they were created to do.

Some people would lament if they saw the sacrifice and the lifestyle these heroes live but for them it is just the "normal" life God has called them to live. And they do it with great joy! It is woven within the very fibers of their being. There is more joy and fulfillment in their lives than one can describe or put into words. I believe this is the abundant life that Jesus talks about in John 10:10. And once your God-dream leads you to this place in your life everything else in the world pales in comparison.

This is the same reason that many sons and daughters of the faith are so bored and discouraged by their walk with God. Either they have bought into the lie that the "abundant life" is only about material things or it does not really exist at all and they are in a state of discouragement over the lack of living abundantly from the world's standards because the enemy deceived them into following something that Jesus never meant for us to follow in the first place!

And when one of their brothers or sisters receives a revelation to take Jesus up on His challenge to live the abundant life there is the resounding cry, "Don't do it!" Yes, more than we would like to admit, often the very first ones to pour water on the fire igniting the dreams of the God-dreamers are those closest to them. Those in their family or even in their congregation are concerned about the dream which they are defining as a fantasy and want to "help" them out by snuffing it out before it can catch fire!

They may not say it out loud but it is a message that has been spoken over and over to courageous dreamers since the days of Joseph. *"Here comes this dreamer!"* And if the initial "shots over the bow" of their heart is not heeded they will turn the up the pressure and do everything they can to persuade the *dreamer* to come back to his or her senses! And this is *within* the church family! It gets much worse if the friends and family do not believe in God! Joseph, of course had it much worse:

"...So Joseph went after his brothers and found them at
Dothan. When they saw him
from a distance and before he came close to them,
they plotted against him to put him
to death. And they said to one another, "Here comes
this dreamer! Now then, come
and let us kill him and throw him into one of the pits;
and we will say," 'A wild
beast devoured him.' Then let us see what will become
of his dreams!"
—Genesis 37:17–20 (NASB)

The brothers of Joseph wanted to kill him along with his dreams! Later we will spend some time talking about the detail of his God-dream but suffice it to say, that the brothers of Joseph were not only jealous of his coat of many colors but *what it actually represented.* They were not threatened by the way Joseph worded his dream but were very threatened by *the impact it would have on their lives.* You see, the *dreamer* will always have a tension with those I call the "dreamless" because the two cannot coexist together. No more than oil and water or light and darkness can.

One is deeply connected to the Spirit of God, and the other is influenced by the spirit of darkness. Those with

God-dreams are connected to God with the spirit of expectancy and have unspeakable hope but those influenced by the spirit of this world have no hope; therefore they find it impossible to dream. Those who are awakened to their God-dream cannot function in darkness any longer. They must be in the Light of God. The deeper they walk into the Light the clearer the dream becomes and it is as if they are living in a completely different dimension. They live by another set of rules. They are grounded by a different set of values and they operate from a totally different perspective. This is the will of God for the dreamer!

So I say, let the dreamers arise and embrace their dreams with such an intense passion that even the dreamless will sit up and take notice! Just like the brothers of Joseph who were awakened to the reality of Joseph's dreams many years later. Yes, may the dreams of God's people be released by the thousands in this generation and awaken those who are in darkness and hopeless today.

Unfortunately the brothers of Joseph were awakened by the reality of the fulfillment of the dream. It does not take faith to be awakened by reality. Anyone can see it then. Well, almost anyone. However, what God is calling us to do is to be awakened by and to live by faith. It is in this reality that we experience the true adventure of walking with God as we embrace our identity and destiny in Christ! This is one of the reasons that God-dreams create a tension for others. When we pursue our God-dream it will always have an impact on others in three ways:

1. It will challenge others to pay attention to the clues of their God-dreams that have been given to them.

2. Others will be challenged to be like you and follow their God-dream and be used as an instrument of God to serve and impact others, which comes from the very heart of God.

3. It will be perceived by some that you are "getting ahead" of others and the natural tendency is to hold you back so that we all remain the same.

The brothers of Joseph were not just threatened by his dream but by the implications of the dream. Let's be very practical now. The coat of many colors was a symbol of tribal leadership and the brothers knew what was coming. The God-dream of Joseph only confirmed what Jacob was already saying and what his brothers already knew in their hearts but did not want to embrace. So, they hated him because of his "dream" simply because it reminded them of what was coming down the road of their future. He was going to lead the tribe when their father died!

It is natural for humans to be threatened when one of their own breaks out of the pack and moves to a new level. It happens all of the time. We do one of two things and both of them are evil. First, we will try to pour water on the dream of our fellow brother or sister to hold them back "for their own good." Or secondly, we will begin to adore and worship them like an idol, and put them on a pedestal which is not helpful at all. You think I am kidding. Just take a look at some churches and how they esteem pastors and leaders like they are some kind of godlike person. And then when one of them fails, falters or falls from grace we act as though the entire world is falling apart. We should do neither of these things. As one father in the faith reminded me long ago, "Every man puts his pants on one leg at a time and every woman puts her shoes on one foot at a time!"

We are all equal in God's sight and we all have God-dreams and we all are human and have faults. God knows and sees them and yet He chooses to work in and through us. We need to take the position to cheer our fellow brothers and sisters in Christ on as they embrace their God-dream! It should never be seen as a threat to us. Nor do we use the world standards to measure the success of a brother or sister in Christ. How can it be?

We are all a part of the same family, the same church and the same Kingdom! When one brother or sister wins with their God-dream we all win! This is why Joseph was willing to say many years later that it was not his brothers who had positioned him in Egypt—it was in fact God so he would be positioned to deliver their entire tribe at such a time as this! God is at work today in the very same way if we would just be awakened to this truth. Wake up! Embrace your God-dream and sound the alarm for those in your sphere of influence to embrace their God-dreams as well. For the time is coming when no one can work and the call of the Kingdom will be over! When we embrace the God-dream we are in fact embracing God Himself! It is to that subject we now turn our attention.

Chapter Five

Giver of Dreams

There will always be dreams grander or humbler

than your own, but

there will never be a dream exactly like your own . . .

for you are unique and more wondrous than you know!

—Linda Staten

And Joseph dreamed a dream, and he told it to his brethren:

and they hated him yet the more.

—Genesis 37:5 (KJV)

Then Joseph had another dream and told his brothers

about it.

"Listen to this dream," he said.

"The sun, moon, and eleven stars bowed low before me!"

—Genesis 37:9 (NLT)

When God gives us dreams, in reality He is giving Himself to us. He is giving us His Heart! In the movie "John Q" a very ordinary man is driven to do the unspeakable when he takes people in an emergency room of a local hospital hostage in order to get a heart and to find a surgeon to operate on his son before he dies. This film creates an incredible dilemma for the audience, because if everyone takes the law in their own hands there would be anarchy. But our heart aches for the family portrayed in this story because they are trapped in a system that threatens the very life of their son, their one and only child. And if they had the right resources he might possibly be saved.

The film takes us through this maze of emotional schizo-phrenia until the moment comes where there is no more time and something must happen before the police storm the hospital and his son dies. So, the father reveals what was in his heart to do the entire time; and that is to take his life and have the doctor take out his own heart and put it inside his son's body! I tell you the first time I saw this film I just about stood up in the theatre and yelled out loud what was screaming inside of me; "This is the promise of God the Father to each and every person on this planet!" God, through Jesus Christ wants to give us a "heart transplant"—His very own Heart so we can be His ambassadors, His representatives, His sons and daughters who grow up to be His fathers and mothers on this planet to touch the lives of every man, woman and child in our generation! This is what God-dreams are all about!

The word "dream" means so many things to different people. In the Bible it simply translates to "revelation." There are over one hundred references to dreams in the Bible. Some of them have to do with false prophets using false dreams and claiming they are from God. So I am not advocating that every dream you have is from God and you should do it. Quite the contrary; if in fact it is a true genuine dream from God then it can handle the tests others will give it and the persecution you most likely encounter from trying to live it. Believe me, in the last couple of decades of ministry I have heard some pretty wacky things and they were all attributed to God. I am not talking about those kinds of things.

However, just because there is counterfeit money does not mean we stop using authentic currency. Just because there are false prophets and apostles does not mean we do not believe that these gifts are alive and well today in our midst. Just because there are false dreams does not mean there are not true God-dreams. In fact, if something is valuable enough to counterfeit it must confirm that there is a genuine somewhere nearby.

Here are some guidelines I use in trying to discern if I am hearing from God when I get dream revelation or any other kind of course correction from God about my life direction:

The God-dream will *never* contradict scriptural wisdom.

The God-dream will bring *peace* to your life even if it conflicts with worldly wisdom.

The God-dream can *stand the test of discernment* and even persecution.

The God-dream will always be *"other focused"* not the other way around.

The God-dream will *take time* to be realized.

The God-dream will only be authentic if you *need God's help* to pull it off. If you can pull it off in your own strength then it is most likely not a true God-dream.

The God-dream will need *wisdom from God* to navigate through the pitfalls and challenges created by it.

The God-dream will most likely *draw fire from the enemy* and anyone he wants to use to attempt to kill it in its infancy.

The God-dream will have both *valleys and mountaintop seasons.*

Joseph's God-dream at the age of seventeen seemed very strange to his family. I believe that the reason the Scriptures say that even after his father challenged him about the description of the dream it says, "And his brothers were jealous of him, *but his father kept the saying in mind*" was an indication of the mystery that had captured the interest of his father (Genesis 37:11). The King James Version quotes the last sentence this way: "but his father *observed* the saying." The word "observed" is translated from the Hebrew word, "shamar" which literally means "properly to *hedge* about (as with thorns), i.e. to *guard*; generally to *protect, attend to*, etc." In other words, something must have rung true in the heart of Jacob concerning this dream. No one knows for sure but since Jacob was obviously planning to make Joseph the tribal leader and he knew the promise God made to Abraham, his grandfather and Isaac, his father, to make their people into a mighty nation; one could easily entertain the notion that something supernatural could be in the making concerning the future of Joseph. Remember, Jacob had his own dream encounter with God when the Almighty "mugged" him one night as he was working through his own dysfunctional relationship with his brother Esau.

My point is this; even if someone like a father does not get on board with your God-dream at first, do not lose heart. God will give full revelation to you in time but he may never reveal it to anyone else until you are actually believing and beginning to live the dream yourself. The question you must answer is: "Do I have the stamina to persevere even if no one else can see what I see from God?"

This creates a dilemma because when it takes time; when you have years where it looks like the God-dream may never come true; there is opposition; even persecution, will you be able to discern the difference between what the enemy wants to do to stop your dream? Will you be able to discern when the enemy is attempting to deceive you into believing some weird fantasy which has been designed to derail you from your true God-dream and ultimately your destiny. How can you know for sure?

The answer is simply, you cannot know immediately. Aha! However, you can know the One who is giving you the dream in the first place and it is that relationship that you must cultivate your entire life in order to have this discernment! And it is this very objective that God has had in mind all along. Your *relationship* with Him as *The DreamWeaver* is much more important than the dream itself! Joseph did it and so can you. The Bible is clear that the God-dream from Joseph was clear enough that he got it, his brothers got it and so did his father. Their reactions to the dream reveals that.

However, because it was not their dream they did not realize that it was much larger than they or even Joseph imagined and instead of the dream threatening their lives and future it was actually going to save their lives and the lives of their families! Not to mention the entire generations after them! Here is what Joseph's two dreams say in context:

*Then Joseph had a dream, and when he told it
to his brothers, they hated him even more. And he said
to them, "Please listen to this dream which I have had;
for behold, **we were binding sheaves in the field, and lo,
my sheaf rose up and also stood erect; and behold, your
sheaves gathered around and bowed down to my sheaf."**
Then his brothers said to him, "Are you actually
going to reign over us? Or are you really going to rule
over us?" So they hated him even more for his dreams and
for his words. Now he had still another dream,
and related it to his brothers, and said, "**Lo, I have had
still another dream; and behold, the sun and the moon
and eleven stars were bowing down to me."**
He related it to his father and to his brothers; and his
father rebuked him and said to him, "What is this dream
that you have had? Shall I and your mother and your
brothers actually come to bow ourselves down
before you to the ground?"*
—Genesis 37:5–10 (NASB)

We all know the answer to Jacob's legitimate question. The answer is "Yes!" Joseph would become the most powerful leader in the most powerful nation of his time. Joseph would not only be a leader, he would become the Prime Minister of the nation, the manager of the King's affairs and his spiritual father! (Genesis 45:8) What does that mean? That means that not only would Joseph's family respect him in this new role but the entire world in his generation. Why? God would use him to preserve the lives of millions of people including his own tribe and the future race of Israel (Genesis 50:20).

This is where it gets really interesting. Some people believe that once they receive the dream and begin to articulate it the magic will happen and—poof! The dream comes true. Sorry, that only happens in fantasy stories, fairy-tales and fables. God-dreams will never come about the way we imagine. How can I say something so definitive? The Bible has story after story of men and women who embraced their God-dream only to discover that the journey from point-A, the revelation of the dream to point-B the fulfillment usually went on paths that they never imagined. It will be no different for us I am sure.

The beauty of the Bible is not only the truth of principles, secrets that unlock the mystery of life and spiritual truth that makes sense of all of the questions we have about our lives and the lives of our fellow travelers on this planet. But the stories and the examples of those who have gone before us not only give us examples of what we are to do and not do but *how we are to navigate the peaks and valleys* of our journey in this great adventure! In this adventure we will encounter storms or what I like to call nightmares. When we travel with God we not only know Him as the

Giver of Dreams but the Killer of Nightmares. Remember Rosa? Let's turn the page and see this revelation.

Chapter Six

Killer of Nightmares

If you lose hope, somehow *you lose the vitality*
that keeps life
moving, *you lose that courage* to be, *that quality* that helps
you go on in spite of it all.
And so today I still have a dream.
-Martin Luther King Jr.

The *nightmares of the wicked come true*;
what the *good people desire, they get.*
—Proverbs 10:24 (MSG)

"I have lost the ability to dream. This country has not only sucked the lifeblood out of me but it has taken my hope from me. How can you dream when you have no hope left? The machine that creates dreams in my heart has also been crushed . . .

. . . I have no dreams."

This is what one Albanian man told me as we sipped Turkish coffee and talked quietly in his apartment about the years that he spent under the dictatorship regime and in prison for not following the strict guidelines of the government. I can still smell the rich coffee, see the lime green paint on the walls and hear the noise of the traffic below his open window. This statement is what I heard more times than I could count inside this country the size of the state of Maryland. Different words but the same message:

"I have no dreams or hope anymore."

For Albanians, the political nightmare they had lived most of their lives had come to an end but the devastation it left behind in the hearts of the people concerned me more than the economic, mental, emotional and physical devastation. Don't get me wrong. Those things are terrible but if a person or a nation for that matter does not know how to dream, how will any of those other things change for the good in the future?

There are dreams and then there are lifelong God-dreams. Even though the topic of this book is about the latter, the former teaches us something. When we have "mini-dream" experiences, they provide clues for us about this whole topic. Our family had the privilege of serving along side many faithful leaders from all over the world in Albania in the early and mid 1990's. In fact, I was privileged to be a member of the original 120 plus leaders who converged in Albania in June, 1991 when the country completely opened up following the death of Enver Hoxoja the dictator who ruled with an iron fist for over 50 years (more about this later). In 1993 I was about to make my next visit to prepare for my family to move there that summer to set up our ministry headquarters for the partnership we were connected to at that time.

I had a strange night dream just before I went to Albania in the spring of 1993 that I was certain was from God but it really frightened me. I was not frightened in the way you would think. I was frightened because I knew that if this was going to really happen I would need to fully engage God in what I believed He was revealing to me by stepping out in faith and risk looking like a fool. When I arrived in the city of Lezhe and met with the believers who met in one of the homes where we planted a church I chose to face my fear head on. I swallowed hard as we ended the meeting and I told them I had something for them to pray about.

They were very eager to hear what I was about to say. You could hear a pin drop. Even the ladies using the hand grinder for the Turkish coffee and preparing snacks in the kitchen stopped what they were doing and looked at me intently. I told them about my dream. In a very low voice I confessed my night dream to them, "I dreamt that I had met the President of Albania, Sali Berisha and God wanted me to share something important with him." Albanians were very respectful and the group of believers I knew in that city were always attentive and courteous to me but on this occasion they began to laugh. Not just a chuckle but a laugh out loud kind of laugh. I did not think it was funny but shrugged it off, and I didn't let them know it annoyed me and asked them to please pray about this. We closed with prayer and the refreshments were served.

I remember telling God in my heart that this is why I was reluctant to share this dream business with other people. As soon as I released that thought in my heart a woman with uncharacteristically long straight blonde hair by the name of Kozeta tapped me on the shoulder and told me something I will never forget: *"Sam, I can help you to arrange a meeting with our president if you would like me to."* Someone else over heard her and began to make fun of her. I encouraged them to stop harassing her as Kozeta and I walked to the hallway near the front door of the apartment to continue our conversation. She had my undivided attention. "Sure, I would love to have your help," I said with excitement. She went on to explain to me that her friend Diana was a student of hers several years earlier when she taught in the local high school. She was currently serving as the Administrative Assistant and Executive Secretary to the first democratically elected president in the history of Albania—Sali Berisha. She told me that Diana was coming to our city the very next morning to go on an outing with her and she could arrange a meeting to set everything up!

I was beside myself with joy and yet I was wondering in the back of my mind, "What in the world will I do if I get the opportunity to meet the President of Albania?" First things first, let's meet Diana and see what happens. I met her the next morning and two days later I was in the capital city, Tirana, standing inside the main door of the Albanian "White House" being patted down for weapons before I was allowed to go in. Kozeta and I went down the long hall of the building where the former dictator had ruled this nation for decades. It was an amazing moment to say the least. The meeting only lasted ten minutes but I gave Diana my business card and told her that I wanted to not only be a help to Albania spiritually but physically as well. I was not only planting churches in their country but I was very actively engaged in helping the schools, hospitals and small businesses. She smiled and put the appointment in President Berisha's schedule for two months later, June 1993, when my family and I would come to this country for the first time together.

I remember walking pass the President's door on my way out and hearing voices from behind and for the first time in my life I began to see the connection between dreams and God and how they can impact other people's lives and even nations. As we walked down the hallway to go back to the exit neither Kozeta nor I said a word. I remember the rays of the sun coming through the window but I do not remember my feet touching the ground. *I was living a God-moment. I was living a mini God-dream! I had been witnessing first hand the way God kills nightmares and gives oppressed people the opportunity to dream again.*

Whenever there is something significant with God and we are committed to partnering with Him in His purposes there will be opposition. A Brazilian missionary to Albania by the name of Najua told me once that she believed the reason that the Albanian people suffered so much was because they were chosen by God to reach the fundamentalist Muslim world. She met an Albanian believer in Brazil in 1974 who said that God told him that the "key" to the fundamentalist Muslim world was Constantinople (modern day Istanbul, Turkey) and the key to Constantinople was Albania. That is a topic for many missiological discussions and another book but over the years I have done some research and found that hundreds of thousands of ethnic Albanians live in and around Istanbul and two other sister cities, and that Turkey is the only country where Albanians could travel freely without a visa, something that many Albanian Christians are taking advantage of today.

The point is that God can and will destroy nightmares and heal the hearts of people and nations to dream again! He is God and He is very good at being God! He is the giver of dreams and the killer of nightmares. But many today equate persecution with missing the plan, purpose and dreams of God but that is not supported by the bible nor the experience of many people embracing their God-dream today. There will be opposition and there will be persecution when you embrace your God-dream!

Persecution does not disqualify the God-dream. I believe persecution is a sign that confirms it! Genesis 37:5 says, "Then Joseph had a dream, and when he told it to his brothers, they *hated* him even more." Some have interpreted this event was caused by the immaturity of Joseph. Some say that if he would have just kept his mouth shut none of the bad things would have happened to him. Some say that it was Joseph's fault all this happened to him. Maybe—or maybe not...

Logical thinking can encourage us to believe that if God has a plan and He uses our dream to guide us toward our destiny and His perfect plan for our lives it would lead us to paradise or at least some form of that. WRONG. The Bible has shown example after example that when we actually pursue our God-dream it will draw fire from the enemies camp—not only natural enemies but God's enemies. These enemies will begin to enlist family, friends and even strangers to try and stop this dream in its infancy. Remember biblical characters like David, Esther, Elijah, Daniel, Joseph & Mary, the Apostles of Jesus, the Apostle Paul and the list goes on and on. Is it coincidence or do persecutions come with the package of God-dreaming?

Look at Jesus and you will see that the God-dream that He embraced led Him not only into continuous persecution, but even into the wilderness. And the wilderness is not only dangerous and the kind of place where we are vulnerable, it is the place where God transforms us so that we can see with His perspective what is really authentic and what is not. It is the place where the "heart transplant" occurs. It is the wilderness place where He gives us His Heart!

Let me take it one step further. Just consider this one last thought of introduction. God-dreams will actually lead us to the very fire that can help us fulfill the dream itself. That fire, the persecution we experience can literally be the "push" we actually need to fulfill the dream in ways we never imagined. If Joseph's brothers did not hate him and his dream they would have never attempted to kill him and eventually sell him into slavery. I am not morbid and I do not wish this kind of experience on myself or anyone for that matter. Yet, we know that this persecution was the "doorway" to his God-dream! Weird isn't it? It doesn't end with his brothers persecuting him. Then he is persecuted by the Egyptians, falsely accused of rape and put into prison for at least 13 years for being moral and righteous and then he was left for dead.

I can just see Joseph right there in his prison cell saying in almost a whisper: "Yes Lord, we are right on schedule. You said I would lead my tribe and my brothers, father and mother would follow my leadership...My brothers hate me, persecuted me, and threaten to kill me, sell me as a slave to the Egyptians, and then because I do the right thing I am put in prison. Not for a few days. No, not a few months. YEARS! 13 years! Yes Lord, we are right on schedule." Did Joseph write anything like that in his journal? We will never know but I wonder if he, like you and I, thought about these kinds of things at times. Especially during those "wilderness" times.

I think there must have been moments during all those years where Joseph wondered about his dream from God. Maybe he even doubted whether he really heard from God at all. Just like you and just like me. This is why it is important for you to remember that persecution does not disqualify the dream. Persecution can purify the dream! It can reposition us to fulfill the dream. It can actually be the power to place us right in crosshairs of fulfilling the actual God-dream itself.

Do not be discouraged. Has your family sold you into slavery? How many of us can say our family sold us into slavery? How many of us have been thrown into prison for doing something moral and righteous? Yes, there are some. Some like Martin Luther King Jr. and those who fought for the Civil Rights Movement and those who fight for the rights of the unborn that are put in jail for their dream. But I am talking about a day to day pursuit of our God-dream. However, many times we experience something of a much less level of difficulty than what our friend Joseph has and we are ready to cry foul and throw in the towel. Is this right?

Do not be discouraged. Even if your family, your friends and your coworkers laugh, ridicule and make fun of you and your God-dream. Pursue it! Never quit! There is a story told of Winston Churchill when he was asked to speak at a graduation ceremony following World War II. When the time came for him to go to the podium to give his speech, he walked up and said these five powerful words: "NEVAH, NEVAH, NEVAH GIVE UP!" Then he walked away, down the steps and left the building. The students and faculty never forgot his speech. Neither have I. Persecution and perseverance are "the twins" dreamers must contend with.

We will come back to this topic of the wilderness in chapter nine. For now, the point I want to nail down is that we need to see the persecution of our dream as something to expect so when it happens we can respond to it appropriately rather than react or even worse quit the journey altogether. This is exactly what the enemy would want us to do. Joseph was not a quitter even though I am sure he was tempted from time to time. When the opportunity came for him to step up into an opportunity he did it. When Pharaoh's baker and wine taster were thrown into prison with him he reached out to them and shared what he had with them. He interpreted their dreams accurately and one was killed and one was restored. The one who was restored forgot about Joseph until that incredible day that Pharaoh needed someone to interpret his dream and the wine taster remembered and they had Joseph brought out of the darkness and into His God-dream! When that happened Joseph was ready to continue on his journey and he persevered until there was a breakthrough. Oh that we could have that kind of perseverance today!

How many God-dreams have been aborted prematurely because the enemy used the persecution and our lack of perseverance to stop us? This is just one of many reasons why God has given us Joseph as a prime example of how to pursue our dream! Tucked away in the middle of the book of Psalm there is an interesting commentary on Joseph and his journey:

Psalm 105:19 (NLT) says:
Until the time came to fulfill his dreams, the Lord tested Joseph's character.

What does "fulfill his dreams" mean? It is referring to the God-dream of Joseph. The word over Joseph's life and the promises of God concerning Joseph was fulfilled in due season. Who knows the mind of God? Who knows when the time comes for your God-dream and mine to be fulfilled? I can only imagine what the naysayers were saying among themselves about the dream of Joseph. Twenty plus years is long enough for anyone to begin to say that it was just a fantasy of a young seventeen year old boy and not really a revelation from God. But the day came for it to be fulfilled. What happened during this long season of waiting?

The Psalmist concludes that the Lord, not the enemy, not fate but the Lord tested Joseph's character! Why would God want to do that? I heard Rick Warren say a few years ago, that "God is more concerned about our character than our comfort!" We are a society that is comfort fixated. Why would God *test* Joseph's character? It did not say "God tempted Joseph's character!" The Hebrew word for "test" is exactly what we would think: "Tsarap," which means "to *fuse* (metal), i.e. *refine* (literal or figurative): cast, (re-) fine (-er), founder, goldsmith, melt, pure, purge away, try." God is always working to make us into His image and one of the ways He does that is to allow the "refiners fire" to work out of us anything that will hinder His plans and purposes for us. And since He knows the end from the beginning and the God-dream fulfilled before it is even revealed to us, He knows what we need to actually live the dream when we finally arrive there!

God knew that His plan for Joseph was to be a world-class leader and in order for him to fulfill that dream he would need a world-class character. So, just a superficial look at Joseph's life would cause anyone to have pity on him. But when you see the entire scope of the God-dream from beginning to end everything makes sense to us. It may not have made sense to Joseph while he was having his "character tested by God" but it would later.

It is the same with you and me. We are in the middle of our journey of pursuing our God-dream and most likely God is doing some character refinement in each one of us! If we have a God-dream at work in us then we must develop the character to fulfill it and for that to happen there is going to be a need for heat! Where else can you find a "cheap source" of heat than persecution and perseverance? These sources will bring any and all dross to the top to be skimmed off and leave God a pure character to release us with into our God-dreams. More on that process later.

Chapter Seven

The Power of Your Dreams

If you can *dream it*, you can *do it*!-

— Walt Disney

It will come about after this that I will

pour out My Spirit on all mankind; and

your sons and daughters will prophesy, your old

men will dream dreams, your young men will see visions.

—Joel 2:28 (NASB)

I was in a deep sleep that fall night in September 1987. I dreamt that I had gone to Africa to serve a Nigerian pastor and his cluster of churches. What was strange was that I was not scheduled to go for almost three more months! It was like I was watching the entire event on a movie screen of my trip to Africa but it was on fast forward. In the dream, I went to Awka, Nigeria and had the time of my life and returned home safely. I woke up and sensed the presence of the Lord strongly in our bedroom around four in the morning and sat straight up in my bed so quickly my wife asked me what was going on. So, I told her what I had dreamed. And then I said to her that, "I was not sure why I would have that dream unless God wanted to tell me something. All I know was that I saw many things that could happen and I came home safely. I was not afraid about my upcoming trip in December so I did not know why I even had it in the first place."

It was right there when my wife began to weep and told me of a fear she was holding in her heart for the upcoming trip and for my safety. So, I told her that I believed the dream was also for her to comfort her and release her from this fear. To this day I believe it was to encourage both her and me because God revealed to us that I went, served and came home safely. After that tender moment we prayed together and experienced the peace of God that is hard to put into words and she just laid there in my arms until we both went back to sleep.

I would later discover that the dream had a twofold purpose. Not only did it bring comfort to my wife before and during that fantastic trip, but it served to open my eyes to how God uses revelation to empower us to serve Him anywhere He calls us to serve. Long story short, when I arrived in Nigeria, my partner and I met many people along the way and something very strange began to happen to me. I recognized the place where we stayed, the streets of the city and faces of several key people. The strangest part of all of that was the fact that "*I had never been to that place or met those people before except for that September night in my dreams.*"

I can count on one hand how many times I have had a dream like that. Revelation can come from God when we are asleep and when we are awake. God can use sleeping dreams, visions, a still small voice, His Word and an array of many other avenues to speak to us and give us revelation. The key is recognizing His voice and then learning everything you can as you walk with Him in this adventure we call abundant living.

The power of your dreams really isn't as mystical as it may sound. Some people really like the mystical topics and others run from it like the plague! It seems that every generation needs to be awakened to the supernatural revelation that God has for His people. His revelation is so important to us as we walk out our adventure with God. It is a constant reminder that His written revelation we call the Bible is so important that we need to spend a lifetime reading, meditating and asking God for a deeper understanding of His Word. While nothing will ever contradict His Written Word and no amount a contemporary revelation will rival it we should not limit God to just the Bible! God is alive and actively engaging us today just as much as He did in Bible times.

The Bible serves as a plumb line for us as we travel this path and embrace our destiny. The truth of God's Word helps us to know Him and His ways intimately and it should serve as a great stimulus causing us to thirst and hunger for Him more and more each and every day of our life. Take the power of dreams for example. As I have mentioned previously, the Bible records actual genuine dreams of His people. It also records those who report dreams that are false and are not from God but from the father of lies, Satan himself. God uses His Word to help us discern and navigate this area carefully. He does not want us to refrain from embracing the power of our dreams just because the enemy tries to use them to deceive us. Satan uses anything he can to deceive us. God is the giver of dreams and since He gives them to us we must embrace them and any other kind of revelation to be encouraged, strengthened and motivated to persevere in the journey God has called each of us to take.

I want to use this chapter to see if I can begin to pull together four key threads I have been alluding to previously to practically help you to tap into the power of your God-given dreams! There is more information we can glean from the life of Joseph than I will ever begin to touch on here. However, the way he embraced both The DreamWeaver and the God-dream of his life is crucial to me and can crystallize a couple of key life lessons. In fact, there are four key life lessons we can glean from the life and example of

Joseph. The purpose here is to provide opportunity for you to discover principles you can use *today* to tap into the power of your God-given dreams!

LESSON #1:
The *preparation* behind the dream means that God is with you!

Psalm 139:16 (NLT)

"You saw me before I was born.
Every day of my life *was recorded in your book.*
Every moment *was laid out before a single day had passed."*

We covered this earlier but I want to make this point crystal clear that God has gone to a lot of trouble to plan your life, where you would live and even give you your name so that it is impossible to believe that the God-dream inside your heart is some kind of accident. Your life is not some accident! You are not some unimportant, insignificant person! You have something special to offer the world and if you do not release your dream and live it we all suffer! We all miss out! The Bible says very clearly that EVERY DAY and EVERY MOMENT of your life were planned before you even took your first breath! Just stop for a moment and allow that truth to sink deep into your soul.

It does not matter what the enemy of our souls has said about you. It does not matter what kids said to you growing up or even family members. Even if you had parents who did not know how to speak blessing and favor over you—God wants you to know that you are significant and your life is important. The desire for you to leave a legacy is not some kind of selfish desire. That desire has been placed inside of you by the fingers of God Himself! This is the reason there is a dream locked up inside of you. That dream in your heart is the compass designed to take you to the destination we call destiny! Just like your fingerprints and your DNA; your God-dream, your vision for your life, your "word from the Lord" is unique and it is extremely important!

Joseph never asked to be placed by his father in the position to lead the family after he was gone. Joseph never asked to have the dreams of being the person who would eventually lead. Joseph never asked for his brothers to be jealous and hate him! In fact, the Bible says in…Acts 7:9 (NLT) *"These sons of Jacob were very jealous of their brother Joseph, and they sold him to be a slave in Egypt. **But God was with him.**"* God was with Joseph! **And God is with you!** The preparation behind the dream is proof that God is with you. Why would God go to all the trouble to write a book about your life, create you to fit His plan and purpose, and put the dream in your heart to lead you into it unless He planned to be with you throughout the entire adventure?

Joseph knew that God had a plan for his life! His great grandfather was Abraham! His grandfather was Isaac and his father was Jacob! He heard the stories first hand that we have read concerning their adventurous walk with God. He knew God had a plan and the dream he had was from God. He did not understand all the details but he knew one thing...*God was with him*! Even though you may experience set backs and disappointments just as Joseph did, you may want to ask yourself this question: Do I trust the plan God has for my life? Every time I am tempted to doubt the dream that God has put in my heart, God comes along and reminds me that He is with me! Are you paying attention to the signposts that God has put in front of you to show you His Presence? They are there! For me, many times, the signposts are my parishioners! When I think about the team, the leaders, the family members, the youth, and even the children in my church family, I open my eyes and see God's presence in them. My doubts evaporate and I roll up my sleeves and continue to work.

What about you? Do you realize that God has a plan and purpose for your life? Do you realize that His preparation in your life propels you towards the dream He placed in your heart? All He has done and planned simply reinforces the fact that GOD IS WITH YOU!

LESSON #2:
Persecution does not disqualify the dream. ***It confirms it!***

Genesis 37:5 (NASB)
"Then Joseph had a dream, and when he told it to his brothers, they hated him even more."

I've already mentioned this in Chapter 6, but it is so important we need to address it again, and push out the principle a step further to put it in its full context and significance. Logical thinking would lead us to believe that if God has a plan and if He uses our dream to guide us toward His perfect plan for us it that it would lead us to a kind of paradise or at least some form of that. WRONG! It will actually lead us ***through the fire***. And in that fire, the persecution and suffering we experience is usually the "push" we need to propel us toward the fulfillment our dream. If Joseph's brothers did not hate him they would never have attempted to kill him and then sell him into slavery. The story doesn't end with his brothers persecuting him. He is persecuted by the Egyptians, put into prison for 13 years for being moral and righteous, and left for dead. I can see Joseph right there in his prison cell saying: "Yes Lord, we are right on schedule. You said I would lead my tribe and my brothers, father and mother would follow my leadership . . . My brothers hate me, persecute me, and threaten to kill me, sell me as a slave to the Egyptians, and then because I do the right thing, I am put in prison. Not for a few days. No-o-o-o-o, not for a few months . . . but YEARS! Thirteen years! Yes Lord, we are right on schedule." NOT!

I think there must have been moments where Joseph wondered about his God-dream. Even doubted whether he really heard from God at all. Just like you and just like me. This is why it is important for you to remember that persecution does not disqualify the dream. IT CONFIRMS IT! This persecution was the doorway to the ultimate fulfillment of Joseph's dream! But it's not what we would have ever expected! And I'm sure Joseph didn't either! Do not be discouraged. Has your family sold you into slavery? Have you been thrown into prison for doing something moral and righteous? Nope, not that bad yet, right? Yet, many times we experience something much less difficult than our friend

Joseph and we are ready to cry foul and throw in the towel. Right? So, don't be discouraged. Even if your family, your friends, and your coworkers laugh, ridicule and make fun of you (and your dream), pursue it! Never quit!

LESSON #3:

Your *path* to fulfilling the dream has peaks and valleys!

Psalm 105:19 (NLT) says something very interesting . . . "Until the time came to fulfill his dreams, *the Lord* tested Joseph's character."

Who tested Joseph's character? WHO? The Lord did. Let's survey Joseph's peaks and valleys for a moment:

- Joseph is given the multi-colored robe and appointed to lead the tribe. (PEAK)
- His brothers become jealous of him and begin to ostracize him (VALLEY)
- He has dreams about his future leadership role. (PEAK)
- His brothers hate him, threaten to kill him and put him in well. (VALLEY)
- His brothers decide not to kill him. (PEAK)
- His brothers sell him into slavery. (VALLEY)

- He is sold to Potiphar and put in charge of his entire estate. (PEAK)
- Potiphar's wife falsely accuses him and he is put in prison for 13 years. (VALLEY)
- Joseph is put in charge of the prison; everything he touches prospers. (PEAK)
- Joseph meets two officials of Pharaoh but he is forgotten for 2 more years. (VALLEY)
- He is called before Pharaoh and made second in command of Egypt. (PEAK)
- His God-dream comes true!

Do you understand the principle here? The path to fulfilling your God-dream is not a straight and level one. Why? Because God is more interested in your maturity than He is in how quick or easy your journey is. Does that surprise you? Does that disappoint you? It should encourage you! Many times we think the valleys are dead ends. Instead of dead ends they are really a part of God's plan to develop your spirit. You can do one of three things at this point:

1. You can choose not to believe it and give up.
2. You can fight it.
3. Or you can open your eyes to this truth and say, "Make me more like you!"

I read a book by Ed Cole recently wherein he stated, "Your character is not defined by what you do when you are alone. It is defined by *what you think about when you are all alone*." What do you brood over, think about, meditate on, and fantasize about? That will reveal the true nature of your character!

Last but not least, our final life lesson from Joseph is . . .

Lesson #4:

Your *perspective* while pursuing the dream is the determining factor of whether it is ever fulfilled!

Many years later Joseph would become one of the most powerful men and leaders in the world. A famine breaks out and Joseph saves Egypt, his family, and the future nation of Israel. His brothers would pass the test and reveal to him that what they did was wrong but would fear for their very lives. And this is what Joseph says to them . . .

Genesis 45:8 (NASB)

"Now, therefore, it was not you who sent me here, but God; and He has made me a father to Pharaoh and lord of all his household and ruler over all the land of Egypt."

Joseph's perspective changed his attitude and it was his attitude that saved his nation, his people and his relationships! His attitude saved him from a life of misery, brokenness and hopelessness. His attitude is what allowed the God-dream to come true! It is the same for you and me. Our attitude towards God and our dream will either lead us into a lifetime of drifting or a lifetime of fulfilling our destiny! God has placed something unique and special inside of you. If you do not release it, you are going to, as my friend, Wayne Cordeiro says, "die rich." It is worth so much. The value is unexplainable. Let me conclude with several seminal ideas Wayne planted in my heart and has now taken root.

Remember, "a dream without faith is simply a fantasy." All true visions from God are drawn from the well of dreams. Prayer and faith turn dreams into vision, and vision paints the picture of the path that you are to walk on to fulfill your destiny here on planet earth! The power of your dreams is incredible. What will you do with your freedom? What will you do with your God-dream? Will you waste it? Or will you release it and run with it? The choice is entirely up to you! First of all start by "*using what you have*". Many times we allow our circumstances to paralyze us from releasing our dreams and fulfilling the God-given plan for our lives.

Don't allow this to happen to you. Start with what you have, and use it! Secondly, "don't worry about what *you don't have* . . ." or waste one more day comparing yourself to your past, to someone else or to the unknown future. Just release that! Lastly, "instead of competing, *start completing*"! I cannot believe how many times we are stopped dead in our tracks because of some petty issue between us and our brothers and sisters. Release it! Work together to complete the Great Commission and reach this world for Christ before it is too late! Amen?

Now, in this moment, ask yourself this question: "What is my God-dream and where am I on the journey of fulfilling my God-given destiny?" Right now, I invite you to acknowledge any area of your life where you feel that you need a breakthrough and to allow God to work freedom into your life. Have you experienced peaks and valleys? Have you lost your perspective? What is keeping you from fulfilling your God-given destiny? Release it! There is power in your dreams!

Chapter Eight

Following Your Dreams
Releases Clues

Twenty years from now you will be more disappointed
by the things that *you didn't do than by the ones you did do.*
So throw off the bowlines. Sail away from the safe harbor.
Catch the trade winds in your sails.
Explore. Dream. Discover.
—Mark Twain

So I have reason to be enthusiastic about all Christ Jesus
has done through me in my service to God. Yet I dare not
boast about anything except what Christ has done through
me, bringing the Gentiles to God by my message and by
the way I worked among them. They were convinced by the
power of miraculous signs and wonders and by the power

of God's Spirit. In this way, I have fully presented the Good News of Christ from Jerusalem all the way to Illyricum.

—Romans 15:17–19 (NLT)

I was walking to the small commuter jet at the Shenandoah Valley Airport. Even with the plane engines running I could hear my two young daughters back at the concourse gate crying and yelling, "*Don't go daddy. Don't go!*" They had overheard my wife and me discussing the headlines of the local newspaper I had tried and failed to hide that morning. I took one last look at them behind the chain link fence and threw them a kiss. One of the businessmen on the flight said jokingly to me, "*They act like you are going to war.*" "*Yes, I know*," is all I said as I wiped a tear from the corner of my eye. How did I end up leaving for this long trip? The fighting that was about to break out in Zagreb, Yugoslavia was real and I wondered how I would get home let alone go onto Albania.

As we taxied down the runway I remembered talking with a friend of mine after we attended a "by invitation only" meeting on the campus of Regent University in Virginia Beach, Virginia. The speaker there was one of the few I had heard of who worked among missionaries to some of the most unaccessible areas of the world. When the doors closed he began sharing with us about the tiny country called Albania. I was pretty good with geography but I did not know exactly where it was located then. The speaker went on to say that at that time Albania "was the most unaccessible nation of the world and no one knew whether there were any followers of Jesus or any religion for that matter within the isolated nation." We listened intently and as we made our way out the door I hit my friend across the chest and said, *"Let's go there!"* *"Where?,"* he responded rather sarcastically. *"To Albania of course! Let's boldly go where no missionary has gone before!"*

I chuckled to myself because as the plane took off I was headed exactly to the country of Albania—if I made it out of the former Yugoslavia alive! Sounds melodramatic I know but it was true and the concerns my wife and I whispered about that morning were more than accurate. I was scheduled to meet with pastors and their wives from all over the former nation called Yugoslavia. My roommate was then the only known Albanian pastor in the world. At that time there were around three million Albanians inside their small country, and about that many in the neighboring area we now called Kosovo. This pastor was serving in the capital city called Pristina.

He and I would have three awesome days of sharing our hearts and dreams. Praying together and watching the events unfold from a hotel bar with the only television in the building that was reporting the breakup of a nation right before our eyes. The plan was for him to travel with me to Albania following the conference we were participating in together. The problems in Yugoslavia would not allow that to ever happen. I would end up catching a ride with a missionary leaving Zagreb who would drop me along the border of Hungary. I would make my way to Budapest to meet my team from the states and we would be a part of making history in the country of Albania.

After some comical events making my way to Budapest I met my team from the states and we headed to the airport. When we approached the counter I knew that the turbulence was going to begin on the ground before we ever took off. As I approached the Malev Airline ticket counter the very smartly dressed and serious agent looked at my itinerary and my passport and then looked up at me and said with a very icy tone and even icier stare, "You're American!" I was not trying to be sarcastic, but responded back and said, "Yes, guilty," with a smile. She did not smile back and responded, "Americans are not allowed in Albania without a visa. Where is your visa?" "Well," I smiled again, "we have a friend in Tirana with our visas." As I prayed under my breath saying to God, "I sure hope she has them."

My friend in Albania was an incredible Dutch/Italian Mennonite missionary by the name of Gesina. Gesina was a very small woman who was a cross between a young "Mother Teresa and Brother Andrew." That is no exaggeration. She had been inside Albania many times and been caught evangelizing during the dangerous days. She was even put in jail for several weeks crossing over the Yugoslavian-Albanian border with contraband (Albanian evangelical tracts). We had made all the arrangements a year earlier and the last time I talked with her was when I was in the states and she was inside Albania getting the necessary visas for my team and me. That was the last I heard from her. Due to the situation with the war breaking out in Zagreb and the antiquated phone system in Albania we would not connect again.

So, back to the Malev ticket counter and the frosty agent. She looked at me one more time and said as though I did not speak proper English, "You're American." Looking puzzled

I said, "Yes, I think we covered that already." She reached under the desk and pushed a button that made no sound but immediately produced a rather large and handsome Hungarian security agent to join us at the counter. They began to talk. When she showed him my passport he startled me (because I was looking at his big gun sticking out of his coat) with the profound statement, "You're American." And we were off to the races again. The security agent went on to explain that if we step off the plane in Tirana we could all be arrested and that he was not joking. At this point I looked back at my team members who were watching all of this and said to me in unison, "Don't you even think of backing out!"

My face must have revealed my thoughts at that moment. This was my dream to go and preach the gospel to a nation who had never heard the name of Jesus before. But my dream could endanger them. One of them was married and had a child. The other members were all single young adults but I was their pastor. And I could possibly be leading them to imprisonment and who knows what else!

They made it crystal clear that we were not turning around now. I had an adventure already in Zagreb and to be totally honest it would not have taken much for me to say, "Okay, let's go home because we have no visas." They were having none of that. They had been praying for nine months and sacrificed a lot to be where we were standing. There was no going back. So, I turned around to face the agents one last time and said, "We believe that Albania is a new country now and we are putting our trust in God."

And with that we were given our boarding passes, ushered onto the plane and were sitting with a rather large group of Albanian passengers who were on their way home. They were so excited to meet Americans and were eager to speak with us. They were asking us questions as though we were something they had never seen before: Americans flying into their country. The reason was we were! I felt like I was shepherd leading sheep. Leading my sheep to the slaughter. I am serious. I felt some serious pressure. Did I hear God's voice? Was this the right time? Was my dream to become a nightmare? Would Gesina meet us as planned? Would we go to jail? Then, with a jolt the plane hit some turbulence and a few minutes later we broke out of the clouds into the sunshine and began our descent. With the descent came an overwhelming sense of God's presence, peace and power!

We landed and I led our team out the door and into this adventure trusting in God and looking for this little missionary woman called Gesina. There she was at the bottom of the steps waiving and smiling with this huge smile! "Sam!" she shouted over all the noise, "You are here!

Welcome to Albania!" Hope began to rise in my heart like a fast elevator! We all greeted her and began our walk to the terminal. I asked her immediately, "Do you have our visas?" "Well . . ." she said, "I have good news and bad news. Which do you want first?" "Bad news and the good news better be really good," I responded. She continued, "I was not able to get the visas we needed . . . however, I have a letter from the minister of culture who is on the president's cabinet and he has given permission for your entire team to enter the country!" I was stunned.

Then, our new friends we met on the plane, a Dutch, a German and an American who we did not know until the plane ride, did not have visas either but had come for the same reason we did. I told Gesina about them and asked if they could join our "team" so they could get in the country too. She smiled and said, "Sure, why not. With God all things are possible." And the fun really began. After several hours of intense dialogue (sounded like arguing to me in Albanian) we were in! We were the last ones to the leave the airport except for the airport employees and rode with them after they turned off all the lights and locked the doors!

The thirty-minute ride to the center of the city passed so swiftly because all of the employees had never met Americans before and they just peppered us with their excellent English questions! The rest as they say is history. Brother Andrew and about 126 other missionaries came from over 20 mission organizations and ten countries. We banded together to share the gospel in song, street preaching, Bible distribution and evangelism everywhere we went and even in the Tirana soccer stadium for a solid week.

When things were winding down in Tirana we held a baptism service and many of those who had put their faith in Christ were water baptized in Lake Tirana behind Tirana University The same minister of culture who had gotten our team in the country was from a city called Lezhe (pronounced "Layz-ya") invited us to do in his city what we just did in Tirana. However, everyone left except for my team and a Youth With A Mission team from Oregon. So, I said, "Sure!" Not really knowing that this city was in the north and had been the place the communists sent Albanians they did not know where else to put when they misbehaved! In other words, it was really the Albanian version of the wild, wild, west; exactly the kind of place we needed to go to preach the gospel!

Well, you can read all about the details in the first chapter of Dr. Howard Foltz's book *"Triumph: Missions Renewal for the Local Church"* where I wrote the first chapter giving all of the particulars. I mention the story here to make the point that the things I learned from that trip and subsequent trips from 1991–1998 trained me in the art of understanding some of the principles of the ways God releases us into our dreams!

Understanding God's plan for releasing you and I into our dreams is both exciting but based on solid biblical principles such as making sure God's agenda is our agenda, releasing our faith even when things look impossible, trusting in God for His resources and the most unlikely people to do some impossible things.

When Joseph was at one of his lowest points from our perspective God was placing him in contact with a key person who would have him ushered into the presence of Pharaoh, the most powerful world leader of his time. This meeting would change his life and the lives of millions forever! In a day everything changed for Joseph. He went from a prison to the palace in one day! He went from the dungeon of despair and the near death of a dream into the dynamic presence of one of the most powerful leaders of his time all because of a dream that God was orchestrating! It was not Pharaoh's dream that brought Joseph to that moment but the God-dream that was given to him when he was seventeen years old! Look at the exact words of this encounter:

Pharaoh sent for Joseph at once, and he was quickly brought from the prison. After he shaved and changed his clothes, he went in and stood before Pharaoh. Then Pharaoh said to Joseph, "I had a dream last night, and no one here can tell me what it means. But I have heard that when you hear about a dream you can interpret it. "It is beyond my power to do this, Joseph replied, but God can tell you what it means and set you at ease.
Genesis 41:14–16 (NLT)

Before I left the country of Albania in June 1991 I had preached side by side with Brother Andrew in morning devotions to the 120 international members serving together as one team. I stood before the city of Lezhe and preached the gospel in the open air with 3,000–5,000 people (one third of the city's population at that time) and witnessed God draw hundreds of people into His Kingdom. I said to myself on the last evening as I watched the Albanian people struggle to get their hands on the Albanian New Testaments that we were giving out, "God, how did this happen? How did you do this? How did our team get to have this privilege to see something that I thought I may never live to see but have now seen it with my own eyes?"

God's response changed my life forever! "*You dreamed it. You followed the clues I gave you and when you were ushered into it you chose to follow Me!*" It was true. I had dreamed that one day, maybe when I was old and gray, I would have the opportunity to preach the gospel to a people who had never heard the name of Jesus before. I would be able to work side by side with other international believers and leaders and make building the Kingdom of God our highest priority. Yes, I was scared along the way and even more so when stepping into the country of Albania itself, but I did not let my emotions make the final decision. I obeyed the leading the Holy Spirit. I knew the day I stepped off the plane in Tirana that I was stepping not only into danger, adventure and the unknown but I was stepping into my destiny! It was and is an indescribable experience. I am not alone! There are many of God's people from Joseph, son of Jacob to Jonathan, friend of David to Joseph, the earthly father of Jesus to many great followers of Jesus as well as you and I who are living this experience!

God is giving us dreams. He is giving us clues that make no sense to anyone else but to you and me as we walk with Him on God-dream journeys! It is exciting. However, there are other experiences we have along the way that the enemy of our soul desires to use to kill the dream before it is ever realized. The enemy whispers in our ear that it is failure but there is another word I like to use. It is called the "wilderness" and to that all important subject we turn our attention to right now.

Are you with me? You have come this far, why not finish the journey. Turn the page and let's jump right into it. You will be glad you did.

Chapter Nine

Embracing Your Wilderness

Dream as if you'll live forever…
live as if you'll die today!
—James Dean

Until the time came to fulfill his dreams,
the Lord tested Joseph's character.
—Psalm 105:19

We were driving somewhere on the "autostrada" as is called in Italian, between Switzerland and Germany when a close friend of mine from Spain told me a story about a Middle Eastern eagle. The story goes something like this. When a mature Middle Eastern eagle gets to a certain stage in its life it will fly into the wilderness and land making it vulnerable to those he would usually hunt. His feathers begin to molt and his beak and claws become brittle and break off. Those the eagle would hunt and eat now have the advantage to turn the hunter into the hunted accept for a strange phenomenon that occurs. Two or sometimes three other eagles will appear seemingly out of no where and begin to circle this eagle in the wilderness. They protect and guard the mature and now vulnerable eagle by day and sit very close by him during the night. They hunt and bring the food to this eagle over a period of several weeks.

After some weeks pass the weak and vulnerable eagle grows new feathers and the broken beak and claws are replaced by bigger and stronger ones. Scientists say that following this transformation the once weak and vulnerable eagle can now fly and soar at higher altitudes than ever before and is a much more powerful foe than before this transformational process occurs. No one really knows how or exactly why these eagles do this and observers are not sure which is the greater miracle of nature—the metamorphosis of the eagle which goes through the wilderness transformational process or the other eagles who normally never travel or live together come and participate in the communal aspect of this radical transition.

I do not know how many times I thought about this story when I went through a season in my own life where it felt as though all my feathers had fallen out and my once strong claws and beak had become brittle and broken off. I too experienced the communal aspect when I attempted to go away into the solitude that the wilderness had called me to but was followed there by several men who hovered over me, loved me, encouraged me, rebuked me and fed me spiritually until

I was once again strong enough to fight the battle that all of us are engaged in.

I had lost my strength and my will to fight. And I thought I had lost my God-dream. I was on the path to fulfilling my dream and had finally came to the realization that the wilderness was a "*normal*" part of the journey. It was there in the wilderness that I came to a whole new revelation of what the God-dream is all about and what a personal relationship with God is all about. It was there in this desolate place that I went through my "heart transplant" and received "a new heart" that would serve me for the rest of my life and most likely into eternity. I call it the genuine "Father Heart of God!"

Many leaders today are trapped with a religious heart instead of tender fathers heart simply because they have either avoided the wilderness altogether or ran from the wilderness by allowing their dream to die; for to them the price was too high. I tried to do both! I attempted to avoid the wilderness because I was afraid of what I would find there. Or to be completely honest, I was afraid of what I wouldn't find.

I was afraid of being in the wilderness because that is the place that only bad people go. It is a place of shame and banishment. And when I was willing to simply quit and let go of my God-dream it seemed and even sounded noble but

I knew and God knew it was the cowards' way out. So I decided to quit fighting the wilderness pull and decided not to quit. I had no idea what was about to happen to me or with me but I went in and made no attempts to turn back.

All of a sudden the Bible looked completely different to me. I seemed to get it now. At least certain themes that were confusing to me and that I had not understood before my wilderness experience now seemed to be coming into focus and there was a crystal clear connection between them. The ancient Old Testament stories of Adam, Eve and Cain who found themselves in the wilderness because of making bad choices or even Job and Noah who had wilderness experiences so that the purposes of God could be worked in and through their lives. There is Abraham and Sarah, Isaac and Rebekah and even Jacob and his wives all have experiences in the wilderness so that God could transform their lives. Joseph of course, Moses, Gideon, Elijah and Elisha continues the pattern. King David's wilderness experience is one of the most famous and we even have his journal which we call the book of Psalms. There are the Old Testament prophets, and then it continues into the New Testament with John the Baptist, Jesus and the Apostle Paul.

There are many different circumstances and reasons for their initial entrance into their various wilderness experiences but one thing is obvious and that is they are completely transformed from who they were when they went in by the time they come out. We also will have different reasons for our entry but if we stay the course we too will be transformed. I believe this with all my heart; you will experience a change so deep and radical that you will see God, His Word, the world and all of your relationships completely different when you come out. Not because they have changed but because YOU have changed.

What signals the entrance into the wilderness? There are no one word answers or sentences for that signal. However your doorway into the wilderness can be triggered by poor choices. It can happen through difficult circumstances with people you are in relationship with. It can happen when people you are close to make poor choices. The betrayal of a spouse or even a close friend can be used of God to take you there. It can be a radical encounter with God that does not line up with your theology much like Saul on the road to Damascus who went to Arabia for three years of "Wilderness 101." He went in Saul and came out totally transformed and when it was complete we would only know him as the Apostle Paul. This chapter is not meant to intimidate or frighten you if you have not yet entered the wilderness. Nor is it to minimize the pain you are experiencing if you are currently entering or enduring your wilderness.

It is my prayer that in some small way God will comfort you by reminding you that you are not alone. Like the eagle who probably thought he was about to die and was surprised by his fellow eagles who just appeared and stayed with him until the process of transformation had moved to the stage where he was no longer vulnerable to his enemies of darkness. God wants to remind you, comfort you and surround you during such a vulnerable time. But He is willing to allow you to go through this process so that the transformation He desires and you and I desperately need and truly want, will be able to occur.

"I do not want to give you this word." My friend Paco said through his tears. "You must," I insisted as we sat on the floor of my church that Sunday evening. He continued, "The Lord says, "You are about to enter into a season where you will be covered by a very dark cloud that will grow into a storm. The storm will be so severe that you will be tempted to believe that the Lord has forsaken you. I am telling you this now so when the storm comes you will know that I am going to be with you and see you through it to the other side where the sun shines again."

To be honest, I was shaken as we cried and prayed together that night. Ministry was happening all around us but it was as though we were all alone instead in a large room with hundreds of people. What did that statement mean? Was I going to lose a loved one? Was something going to happen to my wife or children? Was I going to die? There were many questions but no clear answers to speak of. The real strange thing was that I was not anxious about it at all. I had a peace that whatever was coming, God knew about it and He would see me through it since He was telling me that something huge was just around the corner.

As I reflect on my personal passage into one of the most powerful wilderness experiences of my life it seems obvious to me now. It was not so obvious then but there were signals and clues that some kind of change was inevitable. When our family was serving on the mission field God was calling me into the wilderness but as I said I did not understand that was what was happening and I had no peg in my head to hang that concept on at that time. So, I did the opposite and ran for safety and cover. That was a huge mistake because it is much better to go where you do not want to go voluntarily than to be taken there by force. Without realizing it I had chosen the latter rather than the former.

The long story short I found myself resigning from a ministry role that I had for thirteen years and all of a sudden I was on the outside looking in. The relational circumstances that led me to this point were so painful and unearthed some very sensitive areas in my life that I thought were dead and buried. It was like someone had cut open my chest and did open heart surgery without any anesthesia. I just wanted to quit and get a normal job like everyone else had.

Again, I was trying to avoid the doorway to the wilderness that God was beckoning me to come to. I am not sure when the lights came on and I realized what God was doing and I simply said "Yes, I am willing to go." I believe it was when I was in New Jersey in the home of a dear Chinese-American Pastor. There were several leaders there from Hong Kong, New Zealand and Indonesia.

I told them everything that happened and was making it official that I would not be working with them because of the recent events in my life. It sounded so noble to resign and focus on my marriage and family which definitely needed some attention. But they were not having anything like that. All of these leaders were seasoned warriors in the Kingdom and were empathetic to my season but they knew what I knew deep down in my heart that quitting this relationship was not the answer. So like four stubborn Middle Eastern eagles they refused to budge.

I tried to resist until they began sharing with me some of the challenges they faced when God took them into their wilderness seasons. I was shocked and humbled because I had no idea that they had gone through some of the things they shared with me. So, I submitted to their leadership and it was the beginning of a whole new level of living for me. I felt loved, accepted, forgiven and free to grow in this season I had just entered.

Would I ever I ask to go through it again? No. Will I say it was necessary to bring me to where I am today? Yes. Could there have been a better way to get there? I am sure of it. Like I mentioned earlier I could have gone there when God called me into the wilderness rather than to be driven there. I do not think God is all that concerned about how we get there. He is just going to see to it that it happens because without it we cannot have His heart and we cannot embrace the God-dream He has for us without it.

Joseph's wilderness season began the day he went out to Dothan to visit his brothers...

When they saw him from a distance and before he came close to them, they plotted against him to put him to death.

*And they said to one another, "**Here comes this dreamer!***

"Now then, come and let us kill him and throw him into

one of the pits; and we will say, 'A wild beast devoured

*him.' Then let us see what will become of his **dreams!"***

But Reuben heard this and rescued him out of their hands

and said, "Let us not take his life." Reuben further said to

them, "Shed no blood. Throw him into this pit that is in the

wilderness, but do not lay hands on him" — that he might

rescue him out of their hands, to restore him to his father.

So it came about, when Joseph reached his brothers, that

they stripped Joseph of his tunic, the varicolored tunic that

was on him; and they took him and threw him into the pit.

Now the pit was empty, without any water in it. Then they

sat down to eat a meal. And as they raised their eyes and

looked, behold, a caravan of Ishmaelites was coming from

Gilead, with their camels bearing aromatic gum and balm

and myrrh, on their way to bring them down to Egypt. And

Judah said to his brothers, "What profit is it for us to kill

our brother and cover up his blood? "Come and let us sell

him to the Ishmaelites and not lay our hands on him; for he

is our brother, our own flesh." And his brothers listened to

him. Then some Midianite traders passed by, so they pulled

him up and lifted Joseph out of the pit, and sold him to the

Ishmaelites for twenty shekels of silver. Thus they brought

Joseph into Egypt.

(Genesis 37:18-28) (NASB)

Joseph's entry into his wilderness experience was through the betrayal of his own brothers. They were so threatened by Joseph's role, favor, wisdom and his God-dream that they decided to take matters into their own hands. Remember what I said about people trying to do God's job? Joseph would end up a slave in Egypt but immediately God begins to reveal His favor and wisdom that He has bestowed on Joseph from the very moment his brothers try to circumvent what God was doing.

Reuben felt the responsibility as the oldest brother and intervened for them not to kill him when they took him. Apparently Reuben went somewhere, probably for a walk to clear his head as to what he was to do next. In the meantime, Judah was sensing the heat rising again to actually kill Joseph so he acted quickly to choose the lesser of two evils and sold him to the Midianite traders and at least save his life in Reuben's absence. When Reuben returns he finds out that it has gone from bad to worse and Joseph is now sold and they must do something to cover up what they have done.

So, the story is concocted to make Jacob believe that Joseph was killed by wild animals and the grieving of Jacob's family begins and will not end until Joseph's dream comes true. The dream they were so threatened by would in fact become the vehicle God would use to deliver them physically, spiritually and emotionally. Isn't that amazing? The very thing that seemingly threatened them so much and drove them to commit such a sin against their own brother would in fact be the thing that would eventually deliver them!

It would be a long twenty years for Joseph while he was in captivity but he was not alone in his captivity. Instead of an Egyptian master and later a prison, his brothers would endure the captivity of grief, regret and guilt for betraying one who was innocent. While they meant it for evil, Joseph would later testify that God meant it for good—their good and those of their entire tribe. Even in his absence Joseph's wilderness experience would pave the way for him to become the leader that God had revealed to him to be in his dream. However, his training and placement would come in a way that no one ever imagined. Joseph would *come of age* in a way that no one else imagined!

Chapter Ten

Coming of Age

Dreams are renewable. No matter what our age or
condition, there are still *untapped possibilities
within us* and *new beauty waiting to be born.*
—Dale E. Turner

These sons of Jacob were very jealous of their brother
Joseph, and they sold him to be a slave in Egypt.
*But **God was with him** and **delivered him** from his anguish.
And God **gave him favor** before Pharaoh, king of Egypt.
God also **gave Joseph unusual wisdom**,* so that
Pharaoh appointed him governor over all of Egypt and
put him in charge of all the affairs of the palace.
—Acts 7: 9–10 (NLT)

Now, therefore, it was not you who sent me here,
but God; and He has *made me a father to Pharaoh* and *lord of all his household* and *ruler over all the land of Egypt.*
—Genesis 45:8 (NASB)

J oseph, son of Jacob had a lot going for him and so do you. Steve was a lot like Joseph. He was a regular person like you and me who loved the Lord. He woke up one day not knowing it was going to be his last. The only way to describe young Steve was that you knew that he had a deep love for the Lord and when he spoke to you it was obvious that he spent quality time with God. Some jokingly said that he had the face of an angel. It probably was a relative who started that or maybe it was the fact that he walked to so closely with God that they mistakenly thought he was from heaven. Who knows?

One day he was in the marketplace where people bought and sold goods, drank coffee and did various business trans-actions. And Steve struck up a conversation with a man about recent events in their city. The casual conversation took on a more serious tone and several people standing near by overheard the conversation and joined in the now lively discussion. The lively discussion quickly flared into a one-sided yelling match with all the people except Steve raising their voices. Those yelling were actually on the same side but they were so angry at the fact that the more they tried to put Steve and his opinion down the more frustrated they became.

The small group by now had turned into a mob; there were some serious threats being made and Steve knew this was not going to be a normal day anymore. The mob grabbed him by his clothes and dragged him to a setting that sounds more like a religious kangaroo court and asked him to once again make his defense. And what a defense he made. Steve, also known as Stephen was murdered that day when they could no longer refute what he was saying. His life would make an impact on many including me but a man who witnessed this entire event was actually guarding the clothes of those who would pick up stones to kill Steve. His name was Saul who would very soon have his own encounter with the man Steve was talking about that day that led to his death—Jesus Christ. Saul's encounter was so dramatic it would end up changing his name to the Apostle Paul.

Steve did a masterful job of explaining both the Old Testament and New Testament up to this point in the story and when he got to the historical overview of Joseph, son of Jacob he described, as you read at the beginning of chapter four; the attributes that God gave Joseph and the incredible abilities to live the way he did. There are four things that fueled Joseph's pursuit of his God-dream:

- He gave him His Presence
- He gave him His Deliverance
- He gave him His Favor
- He gave him His Wisdom

These are the same four things that God gave Stephen that day he died. They are the same four things He gave Saul, called the Apostle Paul. And they are the same four things He gives to you and me. It would be very easy for us to take these four things for granted like we do oxygen, water, food and blood.

We do not spend too much time thinking about them unless they are missing and then we cannot think of anything but them. Just bear with me for a moment. If you cut yourself severely and begin to bleed profusely, I mean seriously bleed, everything else going on in your life would pretty much be put on the shelf would it not? Why? Because we instinctively know if we bleed out we're dead. If we go without oxygen for more than let's say 15 seconds, we move into a panic mode and we become preoccupied with the issue. Food and water would take a little longer but not much. However, we do not really think about these four things very often do we? If we are honest, the answer is obviously no, we don't!

As followers of Jesus we kind of take for granted four of God's life giving necessities: His divine presence, His deliverance, His favor and His wisdom until we find ourselves in a situation where it is obvious that we need them. Then we react like we do when we are lacking the four physical necessities of life. We have a similar reaction to placing a cloth on a bleeding wound, swimming up and out of the water struggling for air or looking intensely for food and water when we lack them. When it comes to these four things the Bible describes that both Joseph and Stephen had God's presence, God's Deliverance, God's favor, and God's wisdom.

One morning I got up real early and went fishing in a huge body of water in Chesapeake, Virginia called "Back Bay." My father-in-law and two other men wanted to see if we could catch some big fish that day. We had started out fishing very near the place where we had launched the boat with no luck so we pulled up anchor and decided to cross the bay and find some old duck blinds to see if the fish were hiding there. It would take about fifteen minutes so I sat back and enjoyed the morning sun as it was evaporating the fog over the water in a distance. There was no one to be seen because it was so early. I was excited because I just knew we were going to catch some *big fish. I just knew it.*

It was at this moment I heard one of the men yell over the roar of the boat engine that there was a capsized boat up ahead and two men in the water. I could barely see the front tip of the aluminum boat because it was about 90% under-water. There was one man clinging to the sinking boat and another flailing in the water about 15 yards away. Neither of them looked like they could swim. They were very large African-American men in their mid sixties. We came upon the first man clinging to the boat yelling for us to save them so the men went into action and grabbed our fishnet with a long pole handle to help him.

I still do not remember what I was thinking except that there was an incredible adrenalin rush when my eyes met the eyes of the man going down in the foreground. I took off my shirt and dived into the water. It took me all of five seconds to reach him and he lunged for me. I pushed him back and repeated the words my college instructor drilled into me just months before; "If a drowning person ever gets their hands on you in a panic mode you will both die that day." I pushed him back to his shock and horror and gave him clear unmistakable commands. "If you reach for me again you will drown. Do you hear me? If you lunge for me I cannot help you and you will die today." He swallowed some water and lunged again. I repeated my instructions as he went up and down in his failing doggy paddle panic. Finally he said very weakly that he understood and I dove under the water grabbed his waste and spun him around so that I could grab his left pectoral chest muscle and the hair of his forehead just like I had been trained. He began to struggle and I threatened to let go of him unless he stopped.

He stopped struggling and I took him to the boat. When the other men pulled him up into the boat all I could hear was this one sentence over and over and over; "Thank you Jesus! Thank you Jesus! Thank you Jesus!" They would repeat that heartfelt sentence all the way back to the boat ramp. As we talked with them we discovered that they had been drinking pretty heavily that morning and did not know the Lord. But when their lives were in danger, when the oxygen that we all take for granted was being denied they called out for the Presence of the Living God!

The point is obvious. When we do not walk with God but are lacking the provisions of God and we finally recognize it, we are very quick to seek it! You do not even have to be religious to recognize this. It is obvious to many when they are lacking it. I believe God heard the cry of those two men that morning and we were privileged to be the answer! The four things that God gave Joseph, Stephen, the Apostle Paul and Jesus, He gives to all of us if we desire it. We can deny it but it is available for us and when we have all four synchronized in our lives we are able to navigate to avoid the dream killers and fulfill the God-dream in our lives. Let's take a look at all four of them briefly.

The Presence of God is just that, His Presence. When we know that God is with us we usually describe that as His Peace. But His Presence is when others sense it, know it and begin to describe it. Stephen did that when he described Joseph when he said, "but God was with him." Then there is the Deliverance of God! This is the place when you have done everything possible to move forward in your dream but there is an immovable wall. It is here that God reveals His presence and removes it for you. You can count on it. That is what happened the day that Joseph went from the prison to the palace. It was God's deliverance pure and simple. The time had come and God did what He does best. He is God! He pulls everything together and opens the door to our dream.

Then there is the Favor of God! This is what I call the "unfair advantage." Joseph obviously had the unfair advantage as the Prime Minister of Egypt. He also had the backing of the king and all the leaders subject to the king. This does not mean everyone liked him but he had obviously received the favor of God to do what God intended for him to do. He received favor from his father when he was designated as the new tribal leader. He received favor from Potiphar when he was put in charge of his estate. He received favor even in prison when he was sent there unjustly. And he received favor when he served the nation of Egypt.

The final attribute Stephen pointed out was the Wisdom of God! This is what I call supernatural intelligence that goes beyond human intellect. Joseph had it to guide him all the days of his life. This is why he told his brothers that it was not they who sent him to Egypt but God. And he was not holding their behavior against them. He not only had spiritual insight but supernatural perspective. Exactly what you need to embrace your God-dream and release others into their God-dreams as well. When Joseph came of age these four attributes were working together in harmony. And when you experience them you know that you have come of age and are entering the season of spiritual fatherhood or motherhood and your focus now turns to releasing others into their dreams. It is called releasing and empowering. Let's turn our attention there right now.

Chapter Eleven

Releasing & Empowering

If growing up is the process of creating ideas
and dreams about what life should be,
then maturity is letting go again.
—Mary Beth Danielson

When Joseph's brothers saw that their father was dead,
they said, "What if Joseph should bear a grudge against us
and pay us back in full for all the wrong which we
did to him!" So they sent a message to Joseph, saying,
"Your father charged before he died, saying, 'Thus you
shall say to Joseph, "Please forgive, I beg you, the
transgression of your brothers and their sin, for they did
you wrong."' And now, please forgive the transgression
of the servants of the God of your father."
And Joseph wept when they spoke to him . . .
But Joseph said to them,
"Do not be afraid, for am I in God's place."
—Genesis 50:15–17, 19 (NASB)

We had been married a month over three years when Beverly said what I had been waiting for years to hear. She said just two words that would change our lives forever: "I'm pregnant!" She wanted to wait until I was finished with college and we had more money. I knew we would never have *enough* money to start our family. But things happen and here we were—and I was ecstatic. Over the next few months I told anyone who was even remotely interested and even folks who were not interested at all. When Bev began her eighth month I thought it was impossible for a woman to stretch her stomach to the place where hers was and I was beside myself with joy. I would lay my head gently on her belly and talk to our child. She would playfully push me away and ask, "What in the world are you doing?" I reminded her that our baby was with her 24/7 and knew her voice intimately. I wanted the same opportunity.

Finally the day arrived for our baby to be born and I was ready. I rolled up my sleeves, reviewed in my mind what I had been trained to do La Maze 101, had my notepad and pencil to record the contractions. I was "Roger ready!" I don't remember when or how long we had been at it but I remember when everything changed dramatically. The doctor came in and told us that they were concerned that they were not able to find the baby's heartbeat and the look on my wife's face of terror and unbelief are still etched in my mind like it was only yesterday. I jumped in with all the faith and encouragement I could muster but it would not change what happened. We prayed together and we followed the medical staff's direction carefully. About two hours before the delivery the doctor came in to tell us that he was pretty sure—no, very certain that our baby had died.

It still brings tears to my eyes even though this happened in the summer of 1981. It was like having a bad dream—a nightmare that I could not wake up from. I thought the news was bad but after our baby was born and I went over to the nurse to take her into my arms and hold her I felt robbed. I was devastated. Our daughter was so beautiful. Just the way

I had dreamed. She was round and plump and had chubby little hands with little narrow feet just like her mother.

When I looked and caressed her round face it was obvious that she was created with our DNA. But she was dead and there was absolutely nothing I could do to change it. I held her, kissed her like a fragile piece of crystal and cried just like I am doing right now as I type these words. I guess the pain really never ever goes away. It felt so surreal to me. I do not know how to really describe it except to say that I was having a hard time discerning what was really happening. I was so tired physically and emotionally. Bev had been sedated because she was experiencing something that only mothers can experience when they feel the life of their baby inside of them taken away and she would never rock, nurse or kiss her like she had dreamed.

Once Bev was back in her room and sound asleep, I kissed her on her forehead and walked down the hall and out to my car. The lights were on I am sure but it seemed dark. It was very dark. It was around 1:30 a.m. and our sleepy little town was not making any sound as all. I went home that night to our little apartment and cried in the arms of Bev's parents who had come up for the great event and then called my dad and mom to tell them the sad news.

I could not sleep so I changed into my shorts, t-shirt and running shoes and decided to go for a run hoping that it would help the boulder on my chest to roll off. I ran through the darkness faster and faster as my confusion and sadness turned to disappointment and anger. I wish I could say that I did not have such intense emotions that night but it would not be true. I was so upset and did not know what to do. I ran faster and faster—harder and harder until I could not run anymore and finally fell on to the wet grass and sobbed until I could not sob anymore. I was learning for the first time in my life what grieving was all about.

Ironically I was reading the book of Job for my devotions those days and I had the words of Job's wife still near the surface of my mind when the tempter came and taunted me. "Why don't you follow her advice and curse God?" The voice said inside my head. I was under attack. The most vulnerable time at that point in my walk with God and I was experiencing what the father of lies will do. He will strike you when are most vulnerable and weak. There was so much emotion and anger, confusion and resentment welling up inside of me. So I took a deep breath and yelled as loud as I could in those quiet early morning hours "NO!" And I fell back into the grass and just wept. Then it happened. The peace of God came over me. The power of His presence and

I believe His angelic host were around me pushing the forces of darkness away and shutting the mouth of the accuser. And in a few minutes I felt better.

I will never really know for sure what happened that night in the spiritual realm but what I know for sure is that God would give me the strength to stand with my wife during those difficult days following, carry our daughter's tiny casket to the graveside and pray with a close friend after the dirt and flowers were put in place. Did I struggle after that? Yes. Did we shed tears? Of course we did. But somehow by the grace of God and with the help of our family both natural and spiritual we were able to get through that season of Audrey Faith. Yes, that is her name. The Scripture God gave us really infused life into us then and even today: *"Now faith is the substance of things hoped for the evidence of things not yet seen"* (Hebrews 11:1).

One year later God gave us Rebekah Joy and three years after that He gave us Sarah Denise. We will always hold a special place in our heart for Audrey Faith. Once a child is woven together in the womb of a mother it is never the same again. You can pretend nothing happens and try to go on as though nothing significant happens but life is so precious to God He just does not allow that to be so. And I am delighted He has designed us in this way.

We came to the realization that we had to *release* Audrey Faith and our dream for her life into the hands of God so we could *receive the power* for the next thing God wanted to do in our lives. Like all dreams, some come true in ways that we do not intend for them to come. For us our dream of having a family would be realized by facing the reality that there is life and there is death. There is life after death—new life! And what we took for granted (in our case was a safe delivery of our daughter) we would never take for granted again. In fact, I try not to *take anything* for granted now. I am sure I still do but this is simply the intention of my heart. Both of our daughters have been very healthy and the most dramatic thing we have had to deal with for them health wise growing up was having their tonsils taken out. It felt like major surgery for us because we do not take anything for granted.

We have walked for years with parents who have lost loved ones. Some of our closest friends have lost children through miscarriages and some have children who have chronic disabilities. Yet, we have seen the grace of God in the lives of the parents who had dreams for their families and the children themselves as they embrace God in their own unique way.

God desires for us to find this principle at work within our Kingdom relationships. There is power when we love, dream, release the dream, release those we love into their dreams and take it one step further and find ways to empower them to embrace their dreams the way God empowers us! How do we do this in a very practical way?

We begin by remembering that God does His role better than we do, and He expects us to do our part. His part is the Creator of the Universe Who has a plan and purpose not only for the entire world but for each and every living soul who was created in the womb of a mother. Yet, He expects us to do our part. What part do we play? Well, certainly not His part! Yes, I know that we assent to that in our minds but if we are painfully honest we have at times attempted to at least be the Holy Spirit for someone in our lives. We have sat in judgment over someone else in our heart if not with our mouth. This is where the sin of gossip comes in. We hear some little juicy tidbit about so and so and we add our opinion—our judgment and we have become judge, jury and some extreme cases executioner. Oh maybe not of someone's physical life but of their character. The reasons vary from being so immature to subconsciously believing when someone else is put down we are exalted. The Bible teaches the opposite of that ungodly belief. Or we get caught up and entangled with a spirit of religion who deceives us into thinking that we have a corner on truth and can look down our religious noses upon some poor soul who's gotten him/herself into some kind of mess.

This is not the way of the Kingdom! God desires for us to think the best about someone and when they do lose their way or stumble and fall we need to be the first not the last to step up and help them get back up and onto the path of life! This is what brings life to us! I must admit that I did not come up with this on my own. Joseph, the son of Jacob was one of my biblical mentors who challenged me with this way of thinking.

Here he is living his dream and all is well in Goshen. Except Jacob, the father of Joseph and his brothers is dead. He died a happy man I am sure given the peaks and valleys that his life endured. Yet, like a bad meal, the issue of how Joseph would exact revenge on his brothers for what they had done to Joseph when they sold him into slavery had quickly come to the surface. They did not realize that not only was their father dead but the issue between them and Joseph as well. It had died the day Joseph revealed to them who he really was and had told them again what he said the day his father died: " . . . But Joseph said to them, "*Do not be afraid, for am I in God's place.*" (Genesis 50:19 NASB)

For Joseph the issue was settled long ago. And it was still settled. He knew God. He knew God's role and more importantly he knew his role. If only his brothers would follow Joseph in *his ways* and not just *his days*! They were willing to receive the benefits of *the days* Joseph was living his dream but if they would have just said, "*When I grow up I want to be just like him,*" they would have understood what was happening in their relationship.

We might say, "if they would have had the whole counsel of God, both the Old and New Testaments, the Holy Spirit, the example of Jesus" things would have been different. I do not think so. Why? Because there are people all around us who have access to all of that and more and still act like the issues of forgiveness, believing the best in people and encouraging folks to live their God-dreams does not enter their minds!

Some pastors of local churches are locked into the kind of thinking that limits the very people they are called to serve, when in reality they are there to create and cultivate a biblical environment that releases all of God's people into their dreams and then let God sort out how it all connects. My dear friend and mentor from Hong Kong, Ben Wong, says that our lives collectively should always reflect "*a bouquet of flowers*!" Different lives mean different dreams and gifts but together it makes an incredible image that is unlike anything we have ever seen before!

Wayne Cordeiro was used by God to do many things in my life but one of them was to see *The DreamWeaver* concept from a whole new perspective as a "Dream Releaser!" This is what was stirring in my heart when this chapter was forming in my heart and it is a natural progression to go from seeing your own dream released to then go out and help others to see theirs released as well. Fathers, mothers, teachers, pastors, leaders, executives can get in on this act. Employers can see their business from whole new perspective when they can be used of God to release the dreams of those who work with their company. We can go beyond being kind and generous to being a "dream releaser!" It is to that subject we turn our attention now.

Chapter Twelve

Dream Releasing Revolution!

*Everybody has one. It may be lying undiscovered or as
yet undetected, but everybody has one. It could be broken,
undeveloped or hidden beneath the rubble of past mistakes,
but everybody has one. It might be imprisoned by faulty
character or it could be paralyzed by others disdain.
Still everybody has one. Everybody has a dream.*
—Wayne Cordeiro

The future belongs to those who
Believe in the beauty of *their dreams.*
—Eleanor Roosevelt

And Joseph said to his brothers, "I am about to die,
*but God will surely take care of you, and bring you up
from this land to the land which He promised* on oath
to Abraham, to Isaac and to Jacob."
—Genesis 50:24 (NASB)

It was springtime in Italy when I walked over the very ground overlooking the city called Matera. It was here that Mel Gibson filmed the movie "*The Passion of the Christ.*" There were no famous directors, producers, or actors here on this day. No crowds, only a few others in the distance and me walking around and taking pictures. By the time I got to this spot no one was around. It was the place an Italian bus driver had told me where the crucifixion scene had taken place. There were some beautiful blue wildflowers growing all over the ground. I got down on my knees and laid my camera on the rock to get a direct shot of those flowers. When I knelt down on that spot a memory flashed into my mind.

The theater was packed just as we had hoped! Our congregation was one of hundreds in North America that had reserved a viewing and had invited our family and friends

to see the Mel Gibson film, *"The Passion of the Christ."*
Like everyone else, we had heard the reports, controversy,
endorsements and even judgments of this film before it was
ever released. We had prepared ourselves for the re-enactment
of the brutal suffering and death Jesus Christ had to endure. I
was not prepared for how the film would impact me.

There is one scene in the movie where Jesus is actually
carrying the cross to his death and he stumbles and falls to
the ground in slow motion as his mother is racing around
behind everyone else to get to him and she remembers him
falling as a little boy. The scene climaxes as she finally gets
to his side and he looks at her through his blood-stained hair,
exhaustion and unbelievable pain and says, *"Behold, I make
all things new again."* Gibson obviously takes this quote
from Revelation and uses his creative freedom to insert it
here. I cannot explain it but it hit me like a ton of bricks!

I began to sob to the point that my wife and others with
me noticed. Everyone else had gained composure through
the scenes where Jesus was arrested and beaten brutally.
Apparently all of that combined with the true statement that
he made in that moment coupled with the memory flash of
his being a 100% human, even a child and what was taking
place just made an impact on me. It took me literally days to
recover. Not emotionally. Just from a new fresh

appreciation for what God has done for each and every soul who thirsts for something more than they have in their life right now. My life is not much different than millions of others around the world who can testify of the miracle-working evidence of God making *all things new again* in us! It is one of the greatest mysteries and miracles that many are still unaware of today!

When one stops and thinks about the mystery of how God takes the DNA from two living human beings and creates another person inside the womb of their mother and it naturally creates this person with a specific size, shape, hair and eye color and supernaturally weaves the spiritual destiny and dream for this persons life in there too is just amazing. This is simply amazing but true.

Artists from Mel Gibson in our day to writers in the first century have been trying to capture and communicate the revolution that began when Jesus Christ GAVE His life so that we might have life. It is one of the upside-down principles found throughout the teachings of Jesus. If you give your life away you will find it. It is in the releasing and giving that true life is found. Seems illogical to us in our day and time but it must be true in that this struggle has been around for a long time. Why else would God teach us this from our ancient sacred text?

There are all kinds of revolutions in the history of mankind. Some come and go and others just change hands from one generation to the next. That is what fuels dreams—the hope to change something for the good of people forever! That is my dream! My dream for people in Albania is that they will begin to dream again even though they had their hearts crushed by the cruelty of a dictator. It is now showing signs of new green shoots of life. My dream is also for the billions of people who are seeing the superficiality of consumer goods and what this world has to offer without Christ.

My dreams are for those who are captive in their own nations and are not allowed to travel, let alone dream. My dreams are for those millions who are captive in their own minds with religious thinking rather than The Third Way that Jesus talks about concerning the Kingdom of God! It is the same today as it was when Jesus was revealing His resurrected body and opening the eyes of those who were still blinded from the truth that He came to set every man, woman and child free!

We need to share the love of Christ both with words and deeds and even take it one step further and become spiritual fathers and mothers to those who have been orphaned by their parents, their nation, their religious systems and lovingly create an environment to release their dreams. I wrote this book for one reason and one reason alone and that was to have something to put into the hands of my grandchildren so they would know a little of their grandfather's heart if I was not around to tell them.

You see my grandfather died when I was just ten years old and I was living far away and never even got to be at his funeral. Eight years later I grew up and accepted Jesus Christ as my Lord and Savior and EVERYTHING changed. By that time my grandfather's Bibles, sermon notes, books, journals and everything else vanished. I would give a lot to have just an old Bible of his to see what scriptures he marked that were life giving to him. At this point I have nothing. So, I began to wonder about my grandchildren. What happens when they grow up and turn their hearts toward God and I am gone. What if they wonder about what Grandpa Scaggs believed? What if they wanted to know what my life message was? So, I wrote this for them. As the word got out many of my friends around the world asked me to give them a copy because they have heard me talk a lot about the things I have written in this book. I submit this to you with the hope and trust that you will be encouraged to walk with The One and Only DreamWeaver!

The DreamWeaver is the same yesterday, today and forever! Give your heart completely to Him and ask Him to reveal His Dream for you! Ask Him to reveal the plan He has for your life! You only have one life to GIVE! Give it in such a way that when are lying in your bed taking your last breath you can always say, "every man dies but not every man truly lives!" I have lived! I have given my life so that others may find life in Him! Live your God-dream to the fullest! May God's hand be upon you all the days of your life. Amen.

Epilogue

"If we don't have our *dreams, we have nothing!*"

-Rocket Man, Charlie Farmer

There is no way on earth I could end this book without mentioning the major motion picture released in 2007 called "*The Astronaut Farmer!*" I was actually hidden away in the mountains of Bath County, Virginia for three weeks to write the first draft of "The DreamWeaver" manuscript when I needed a break and went down to the country store that had the only collection of video and DVD rentals in town (no kidding). And there it was on the shelf.

If you haven't seen it yet let me spoil it for you! Charlie Farmer is a regular guy who had a big dream! His dream was to build a rocket and orbit the earth and return home safely. It is a fantastic family film that depicts in a very short span of ninety minutes that there is power in your dreams. He is no pushover. He is an astrophysicist whose dream goes through some valleys and set backs but he persisted. And when the whole world turned against him his life partner, best friend and wife helped him to take the final step needed to go to outer space!

When he unveiled his second rocket with the name *"Dreamer"* I just about fell onto the floor! His entire family got into the act and they pulled something off far beyond the story line—they communicate through modern story telling a wonderful example of what I have been trying to say all along. *"If we don't have our dreams, we have nothing!"* Dream dreams so big and hairy, so audacious and outlandish that the only way they can come true is that people will say "God help you!" Because that is exactly what He is waiting to do! He is the One who weaved it into your heart in the first place and He is the One who wants to empower you to see it through to the end. The only thing that can stop you is YOU! The enemy of God can try to deceive you and the dreamless can try to taunt you and discourage you. But with God, your Father in Heaven, you can do anything!

So, do not let anyone tell you different. Dream God Sized Dreams for His Glory and change this world into a better place. What can one person do? Amazing things when you stop and think about it—you may not change the entire world by yourself but you can change it for at least one! And if each one of us could adopt that simple philosophy with a "can do" attitude full of faith in God we could see this world changed forever!

Let them say this about you—*"Here comes that dreamer!"*

About the Author

Sammy Ray Scaggs is an author, pastor, missionary and speaker. He has traveled to over 90 nations and has been speaking to audiences in most of those places. Sam is currently serving as Co-Pastor of Mt. Pleasant Mennonite Church, where he found the Lord in 1976 and is the Vice President & International Director for Lifeforming Leadership Coaching which trains leaders globally to unlock their dreams and live them! Sam lives on the east coast of Virginia with his wife, Beverly, very close to his two married daughters, their husbands and two grandsons. He loves to travel, fish, photography and spending as much time with his family as possible.

To contact Sam about seminars, audio tapes and other resources just visit:

www.Ps139DreamWeaver.com

Breinigsville, PA USA
11 January 2010
230564BV00001B/2/P